Please sir
Can I have some more?
— Oliver Twist

Oleander Press
16 Orchard Street
Cambridge
CB1 1JT

www.oleanderpress.com

This edition published: 2013

A CIP catalogue record for the book is available from the British Library.

Cover photo courtesy of Archant Suffolk

ISBN: 9781909349971

Words, design, typeset and photography by James and Liz Archer
james@coastlinegraphics.co.uk

Printed by Coastline Graphics on sustainably sourced paper

www.olivers-kitchen.co.uk   Twitter: @ollieskitchen   www.facebook.com/oliverskitchen

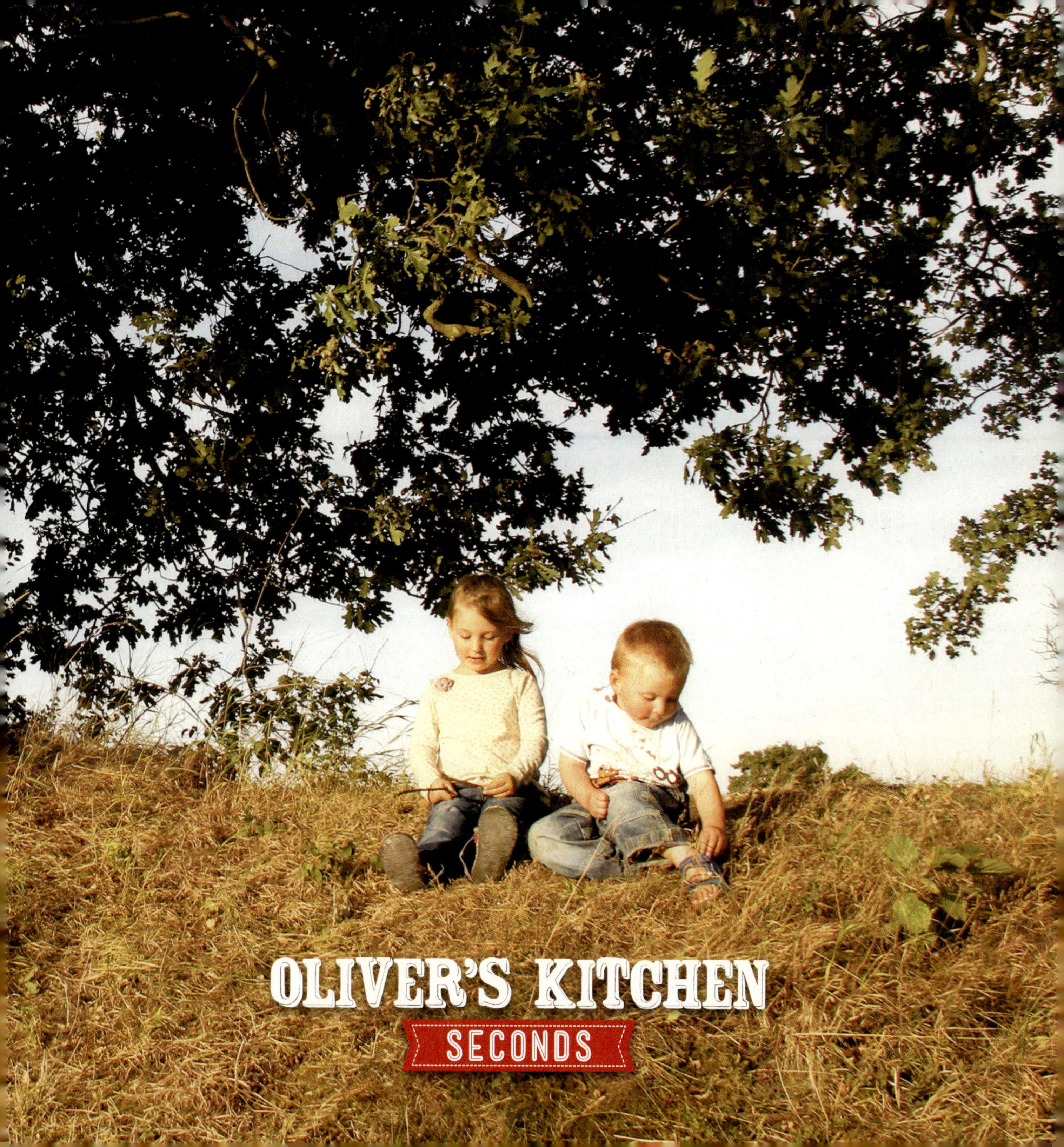
OLIVER'S KITCHEN
SECONDS

OLIVER'S KITCHEN

SECONDS

SPECIAL

LIMITED

EDITION

A FOREWORD BY
JAMIE OLIVER

Hi guys,

Although strokes have affected my family, I was never aware of childhood strokes until I heard little Ollie's story, and since then I've been following his journey with real pride and admiration, and I'm very happy to have been asked to write a foreword for this lovely little book.

You only have to look at it to see that it has been put together by a wonderful, loving family, and I think that the pictures say it all. There's a whole range of recipes in this book that will take you from comfort food and super-naughty home-baked sweet treats to jams, salads and lots of family favourites. It's laid out simply, super easy to use, and most importantly, you can tell it's authentic – and not all books can say that!

Enjoy this wonderful book and have a whole lot of fun. And, anything you can do to raise awareness or to help out with fundraising would be amazing.

Big love

Jamie O
xxx

CONTENTS

7 Foreword   9 Introduction

❧ SPRING ❧

12 Cheese Scones
16 Shortbread Cookies
20 Mia's Rainbow Cake
24 Giant Scotch Eggs

28 Ollie's Dinosaur Cake
32 Chocolate Mousse
36 Homemade Quiche
40 Cake Pops

❧ SUMMER ❧

46 Eton Mess
50 Goat's Cheese Salad
52 Cherry Cordial
54 Spanish Omelette

58 Teeny Cheesecakes
62 Homemade Burgers
66 Mia's Strawberry Jam
70 Homemade Lemonade

❧ AUTUMN ❧

80 Toffee Apples
84 Grannie's Fudge
88 Tiramisu
92 Glitter Plum Jam

96 Fridge Cake
102 Pineapple Upside Down Cake
106 Homemade Pizza
110 Banoffee Pie

❧ WINTER ❧

116 Roasted Onion Soup
120 Jam Roly Poly
124 Mexican Eggs
128 Chocolate Brownies

132 Ratatouille
136 Candy Cane Reindeers
138 Sticky Toffee Pudding
142 Redcurrant Jelly

INTRODUCTION
BY MUM AND DAD

Firstly we would like to thank you for your support. As you may know, Oliver suffered a stroke when he was being born in hospital. We have included more of his recovery progress in this book as well as suggesting some fund raising ideas that you may wish to try. We have been blessed with some of the most outstanding support, help and encouragement over the last few years and for this we are extremely grateful. We found that helping some great causes and turning a pretty frightening situation into a more positive one can be incredibly healing and rewarding as well as a lot of fun!

As with the first book, all of the profits made by making this book are being donated to two incredible charities that have helped us through the hard times. West Suffolk Hospital, where Oliver and Mia were born is the first to benefit with the funds being donated to it's neonatal unit. The Stroke Association is the other charity to benefit from the funds raised and we hope they can continue their fantastic work helping others who have been affected by strokes.

We created Oliver's Kitchen for two reasons; to encourage fun, family cooking and to raise funds and awareness of childhood stroke. The response the first book was met with was incredible and we won't lie, we had a whole lot of fun making it, promoting it and doing fund raising events!

We firmly believe that cooking can be enjoyed by the whole family and we don't just mean the eating part! There are certain parts that need to be left to us "big people" but most of the fun bits of cooking and preparation can be enjoyed by the little ones too.

In this book we explore different types of cooking with the foundation being that the recipes should be fun and the food should be tasty! We make seasonal recipes like tasty soups and jam roly polys along with novelty recipes like cake pops and toffee apples. Mia makes a variety of special jams and jellies and there are some family favourites and classics like traditional homemade lemonade!

Enjoy x

SPRING

Spring is a fantastic time of year, full of freshness!

- -

I LOVE SPRING TIME! WITH ALL THE FRESH NEW LIFE AND COLOURS IT REALLY IS A BEAUTIFUL TIME OF YEAR.

HERE WE HAVE A SELECTION OF REFRESHING RECIPES TO GET YOU RIGHT INTO THE SWING OF SPRING! EASTER HAS TO BE ONE OF THE MAIN SPRINGTIME EVENTS AND IT IS JUST FULL OF GREAT REASONS TO GET INTO THE KITCHEN! WE HAVE A VARIETY OF DISHES FROM GIANT SCOTCH EGGS TO CHEESY SCONES AND SHORTBREAD COOKIES, SOMETHING FOR EVERYONE.

SO ENJOY THIS SEASON AND ALL THE BOUNTY IT HAS TO OFFER.

- CHEESE SCONES
- SHORTBREAD COOKIES
- MIA'S RAINBOW CAKE
- GIANT SCOTCH EGGS
- OLLIE'S DINOSAUR CAKE
- CHOCOLATE MOUSSE
- MUMMY'S QUICHE
- CAKE POPS

DELICIOUS CHEESY SCONES

What a perfect little lunch time snack, easy to make too!

This delicious recipe was kindly given to us by a lovely lady named Carol. Daddy made them one day and we realised what all the fuss was about!

YOU WILL NEED:

200G SELF RAISING FLOUR
50G BUTTER
3OZ STRONG CHEESE
1OZ GRATED ITALIAN CHEESE
100ML MILK
PINCH OF SALT

1. FIRST YOU NEED TO SIFT THE FLOUR AND SALT TOGETHER AND MIX WITH THE BUTTER TO FORM LOOSE BREADCRUMBS. OH AND WHILE YOU ARE DOING THIS, GET A BIG PERSON TO PRE-HEAT THE OVEN TO 220°C.

2. ADD THE STRONG CHEESE AND MIX AGAIN. TIME TO GET MESSY!

3. ADD THE MILK THEN KNEAD THIS INTO A SOFT DOUGH. I ASKED MIA TO HELP WITH THIS BIT.

4. THEN GET THE OLD ROLLING PIN OUT AND ROLL THE DOUGH OUT TO ABOUT 1 INCH THICK. THE THICKNESS OF ONE OF OUR SHAPE CUTTERS.
CUT THE DOUGH INTO SHAPES. YOU CAN USE ANY SHAPES FOR THIS I USED CIRLCES AND FLOWER SHAPES TO KEEP MIA HAPPY!

5. POP THE SHAPES ONTO A BAKING TRAY AND BRUSH WITH SOME MILK. TOP THEM WITH THE GRATED ITALIAN CHEESE AND PLACE ON THE MIDDLE SHELF OF THE OVEN FOR 10-15 MINS.

ONCE THEY ARE COOKED, LET THEM COOL FOR 5 MINS AND ENJOY! (MR LEOPARD LOVES THEM SO MUCH!)

Mr Leopard

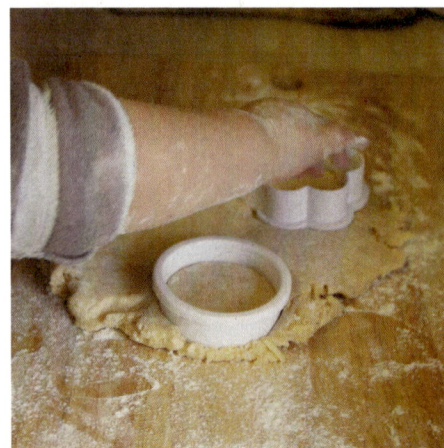

SHORTBREAD COOKIES

Delicious shortbread cookies, perfect with a cup of tea!

Prep 20 MINS
Cooking 10–30 MINS

These naughty treats are best served with a nice cup of tea as they make great dunkers! We made these as a treat for mummy on Mothers Day! We made a heart shaped one with an edible flower on top to decorate! We were in mummy's good books for ages!

YOU WILL NEED:

125G SOFTENED BUTTER
55G CASTER SUGAR
150G PLAIN FLOUR

1. IF YOU ARE MAKING THESE AS A TREAT THEN MAKE SURE THE RECIPIENT IS WELL OUT OF THE WAY!

YOU WILL HOWEVER NEED TO FIND ANOTHER BIG PERSON TO PREHEAT THE OVEN TO 160°C.

2. NOW GET ALL YOUR INGREDIENTS READY THEN CREAM TOGETHER THE BUTTER AND SUGAR IN A BIG OLD BOWL.

3. SLOWLY ADD THE FLOUR AND MIX IT IN NICELY. THIS WILL SLOWLY BECOME A BALL SO KEEP WORKING IT UNTIL IT ENDS UP A SMOOTH FIRM BALL OF GOODNESS.

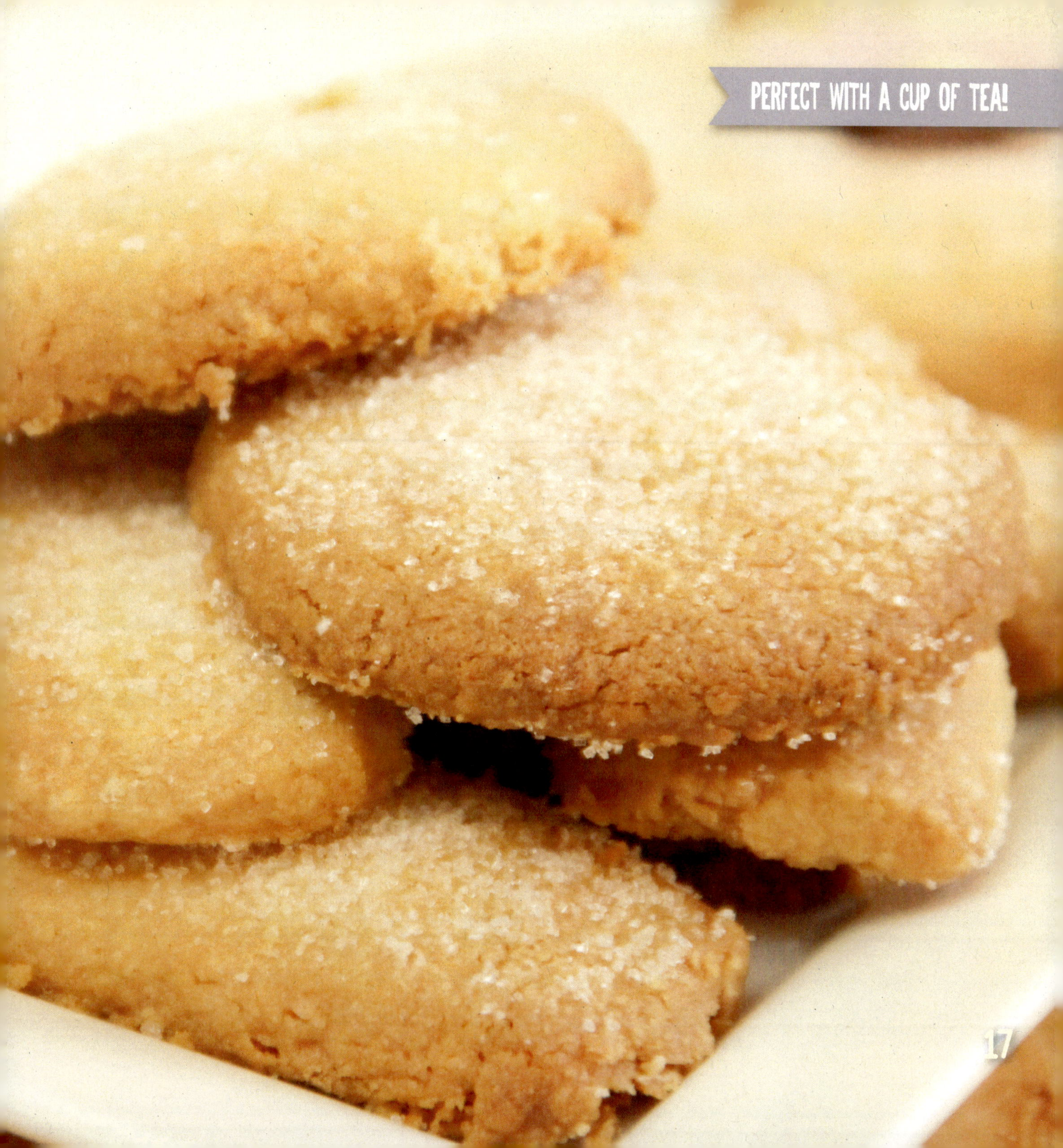
PERFECT WITH A CUP OF TEA!

4. NOW CLEAR A SURFACE READY FOR ROLLING! PLOP THE DOUGH ONTO THE FLOURED SURFACE AND START ROLLING IT OUT. IT WANTS TO BE ABOUT 1/2 CM THICK WHEN YOU ARE DONE. THIS CAN BE A BIT TRICKY SO ASK FOR HELP IF YOU NEED IT.

5. YOU NOW NEED TO CUT THEM INTO SHAPES. YOU CAN USE ANY SHAPE YOU LIKE. THERE ARE LOTS OF SHAPED PASTRY CUTTERS AVAILABLE OR YOU CAN JUST CUT THEM OUT YOURSELF. GET A BIG PERSON TO USE A SHARP KNIFE OR TRY WITH A BLUNT PLASTIC ONE YOURSELF. THEY DON'T MAKE IT EASY FOR US LITTLE FOLK!

6. NOW GET YOUR BIG PERSON TO POP THEM IN THE OVEN FOR ABOUT 10-15 MINS.

WHILE THEY ARE COOKING YOU CAN GET THE SUGAR READY FOR DUSTING. IT IS BEST TO HAVE A QUICK TASTE OF THE SUGAR, JUST TO MAKE SURE IT IS OK.

WHEN THEY ARE READY TO COME OUT, LET THEM COOL FOR A LITTLE WHILE AS THEY WILL BE HOT. THEN DUST THEM WITH SOME SUGAR TO MAKE THEM LOOK TRULY IRRESISTIBLE!

POP THE KETTLE ON AND GO AND SURPRISE SOMEONE WITH A DELICIOUS LITTLE BRITISH TREAT! OR IF YOU'RE A BIT GREEDY, GO NUTS AND SCOFF THE LOT!

MIA'S RAINBOW BIRTHDAY CAKE

Prep: **30 MINS**
Cooking: **50 MINS**

A multi layered, colourful, delicious cake topped with unicorns!

Although this may look complicated, it is a surprisingly easy recipe. You basically makes lots of thin sponge cakes coloured to your choice then stack them all up.

YOU WILL NEED:

FOR THE CAKE:
200G CASTER SUGAR
200G BUTTER
200G SELF RAISING FLOUR
4 FREE RANGE EGGS
1 TEASPOON BAKING POWDER
2 TABLESPOONS MILK
A FEW DROPS OF YOUR CHOSEN FOOD COLOURS

SOME (OPTIONAL) UNICORNS AS DECORATIONS

FOR THE FILLING:
100G BUTTER
140G ICING SUGAR
A FEW DROPS OF VANILLA EXTRACT

1. TO START WITH MAKE A SPONGE MIX BY MIXING THE BUTTER, SUGAR AND EGGS TOGETHER. AFTER A FEW MINUTES ADD THE FLOUR, BAKING POWDER AND MILK AND GIVE IT ALL A GOOD MIX UNTIL SMOOTH.

2. ASK A BIG PERSON TO PREHEAT THE OVEN TO 190°C WHILST YOU GREASE A BAKING TIN WITH BUTTER. THE TIN CAN BE A NORMAL ONE OR YOU CAN USE A SHAPED TIN LIKE THE NUMBER 5 FOR EXAMPLE. THESE ARE AVAILABLE TO HIRE FOR A FEW DAYS WHICH WORKS OUT CHEAPER UNLESS YOU HAVE LOTS OF 4 YEARS OLDS ABOUT TO REACH THEIR NEXT BIRTHDAY!

3. NOW DIVIDE THE MIXTURE INTO THE NUMBER OF COLOURED LAYERS THAT YOU WANT YOUR CAKE TO HAVE. WE ARE DOING 5 SO DIVIDE THE MIX INTO 5 BOWLS AND ADD A FEW DROPS OF DIFFERENT COLOURED FOOD COLOURING TO EACH BOWL. SO WE ENDED UP WITH 5 DIFFERENT COLOURED CAKE MIXES.

4. THIS BIT TAKES A BIT OF TIME BUT IS WORTH IT. WE NOW POUR 1 OF THE MIXES INTO THE TIN AND BAKE FOR 10 MINS. YOU CAN CHECK IT'S DONE BY POKING A KNIFE IN THE CAKE AND SEEING IF IT COMES OUT CLEAN.

IF IT DOES THEN IT IS DONE. THESE THIN CAKES WON'T TAKE LONG TO COOK SO KEEP AN EYE ON THEM.

5. REPEAT THIS WITH ALL OF THE COLOURED MIXES AND PLACE EACH BAKED CAKE ON THE SIDE TO COOL ONCE THEY ARE DONE.

6. NOW LET'S MAKE THE ICING. AS WITH THE SPONGES, YOU MAY NEED TO MAKE MORE DEPENDING ON THE SIZE OF YOUR CAKE TINS.
BEAT THE BUTTER UNTIL IT'S SMOOTH AND GRADUALLY ADD THE ICING SUGAR. ADD A FEW DROPS OF THE VANILLA EXTRACT AND MIX UNTIL IT IS NICELY SMOOTH AND SPREADABLE. THIS CAN NOW BE USED BETWEEN THE LAYERS OF THE CAKE AS YOU STACK THE DIFFERENT COLOURED SPONGES ON TOP OF EACH OTHER.

7. ONCE YOUR CAKE IS SUITABLY TALL YOU CAN SPREAD THE REMAINING ICING OVER THE OUTSIDE TO HIDE THOSE BEAUTIFUL COLOURS, ONLY TO BE REVEALED WHEN YOU CUT THE CAKE! SPRINKLE OVER SOME HUNDREDS AND THOUSANDS AND IT'S READY FOR THE CANDLES AND OF COURSE, THE UNICORNS!

Unicorn

23

SUPER GIANT SCOTCH EGGS

A tasty treat made using delicious local goose eggs

After visiting and putting on a small cake stand at a local Farm Shop during their annual food festival we came across some huge geese eggs for sale. So we stocked up, took them home and decided to make mahoosive scotch eggs!

YOU WILL NEED:

- 2 LARGE FREE-RANGE GOOSE EGGS
- 275G SAUSAGE MEAT (MAYBE MORE)
- 4 RASHERS OF SMOKED BACON
- 1 TSP FRESH THYME LEAVES
- 1 TBSP CHOPPED FRESH PARSLEY
- 1/2 ONION, VERY FINELY CHOPPED
- SALT AND FRESHLY GROUND BLACK PEPPER
- 125G/4OZ PLAIN FLOUR
- 1 FREE-RANGE EGG, BEATEN
- 125G/4OZ BREADCRUMBS

1. RIGHT NOW THIS RECIPE I WILL BE HONEST IS NOT AN EXACT SCIENCE! WE HAD NOT MADE SCOTCH EGGS BEFORE WITH BIG OLD GOOSE EGGS SO WE KIND OF GUESSED AS WE WENT!
FIRST WE HARD BOILED THE EGGS WHICH PROBABLY TOOK ABOUT 12 MINUTES! IT SEEMED FOREVER!

2. WHILST THESE WERE BOILING I ASKED A BIG PERSON TO FRY OFF THE BACON UNTIL NICE AND CRISPY. BACON GOES SO WELL WITH EGGS!

3. THEN WHEN THE BACON IS DONE WE FINELY CHOPPED IT UP. BY THIS TIME THE EGGS WERE READY SO WE DRAINED THEM AND LET THEM COOL IN COLD WATER.

GOOSE EGGS ARE GREAT!

4. AFTER PEELING THE SHELLS OFF THE EGGS IT IS TIME TO PREPARE THE SAUSAGE MEATY PART. FOR THIS WE NEED TO MIX THE SAUSAGE MEAT UP WITH THE THYME, PARSLEY AND CHOPPED ONION ALONG WITH SOME GOOD SEASONING OF SALT AND PEPPER.

5. DIVIDE THE SAUSAGE MEAT MIXTURE INTO 2 AND MAKE THEM INTO ROUGH OVAL SHAPES. THEN ADD A SMALL HEAP OF THE CHOPPED BACON.

6. ADD THE FLOUR TO A BOWL AND SEASON WITH SALT AND PEPPER. THEN DIP THE EGGS INTO IT AND POP THEM ON TOP OF THE PILE OF BACON.

7. NOW WE WRAP THE SAUSAGE MEAT AROUND THE EGG MAKING SURE THAT THE WHOLE EGG IS COVERED AND NICE AND SMOOTH.

IT IS LIKE A MEATY SHELL FOR THE EGG!

8. NOW THAT WE HAVE A PAIR OF MEATY EGGS WE NEED TO BRUSH THEM WITH BEATEN EGG AND ROLL THEM AROUND IN THE BREADCRUMBS. MAKE SURE YOU GET THEM COMPLETELY COVERED SO KEEP ROLLING THEM AROUND AND AROUND!

9. ONCE THEY ARE ALL CRUMBY IT IS TIME TO GET THAT BIG PERSON WHO IS ON STANDBY TO POP THEM INTO A PRE-HEATED OVEN (180°C) FOR ABOUT 35 MINUTES UNTIL THEY ARE BEAUTIFULLY GOLDEN BROWN.

10. ONCE COOKED AND REMOVED FROM THE OVEN, LET THEM COOL FOR 5 MINUTES AND ENJOY!

THESE ARE PERFECT FOR LUNCHES OR MAYBE AS PART OF A PICNIC?!

27

MY CHOCOLATE DINOSAUR CAKE

my second ever birthday cake and it's grrreeeat!

Well it is my second birthday and guess what..... I'm making my own cake! Is that right? Should that be allowed? Something is definitely wrong here! Well, nevermind, I do a better job myself anyway and so will you if you follow this tasty recipe!

YOU WILL NEED:

250G SELF RAISING FLOUR
250G SOFT BROWN SUGAR
250G BUTTER
250G PLAIN CHOCOLATE
40G COCOA
4 FREE RANGE EGGS

300ML POT OF SINGLE CREAM
25G BUTTER
150-200G ICING SUGAR

1 PACK OF ROLL OUT ICING

1. GET THOSE LAZY BIG PEOPLE TO PREHEAT THE OVEN TO 150°C THEN THEY CAN GO AWAY!

2. NOW MEASURE OUT THE INGREDIENTS AND MIX THE FLOUR, SUGAR AND COCOA TOGETHER INTO A BOWL.

3. BOTHER, WE NEED THE BIG PEOPLE AGAIN. GO GET THEM AND ASK THEM TO MELT THE BUTTER AND CHOCOLATE TOGETHER WITH 200ML OF WATER OVER A PAN OF BOILING WATER.

THEN BEAT THIS INTO THE FLOUR/ SUGAR MIX AND ADD THE EGGS. GIVE THIS A GOOD STIR THEN POUR INTO A CAKE TIN AND BAKE FOR 1 HOUR.

29

4. TO MAKE THE ICING WE NEED TO MELT THE BUTTER AND ADD THE CREAM. LET THIS COOL FOR A WHILE AND ADD ENOUGH ICING SUGAR TO MAKE IT STIFF BUT SPREADABLE.

5. ONCE THE CAKE IS DONE, SLICE IT IN HALF AND SPREAD THE ICING BETWEEN THE LAYERS.

6. NOW THE FUN BIT, YOU NEED TO SHAPE YOUR CAKE TO A ROUGH DINOSAUR SHAPE. REMEMBER TO PICK YOUR FAVOURITE DINOSAUR BEFORE HAND. ONCE THE CAKE ROUGHLY (KIND OF) RESEMBLES A DINOSAUR SHAPE THEN ROLL OUT THE ROLL-OUT ICING AND LAY OVER THE TOP OF THE CAKE. IT IS BEST TO DO THIS ON THE BOARD OR PLATE YOU INTEND TO LEAVE THE CAKE ON SO THERE'S NO NEED TO MOVE IT ABOUT.

7. PRETEND LIKE YOUR PLAYING WITH PLAY-DOH AND MOULD THE CAKE INTO YOUR DESIRED SHAPE. THEN MAKE SURE IT HAS THE ESSENTIALS – EYES, NOSTRILS, TONGUE, MOUTH, SPIKES, TAIL, TEETH, KNEES ETC THEN HEAD OFF AND OPEN YOUR PRESENTS! (THAT PART MAY JUST BE FOR ME!)

CHOCOLATE MOUSSE

Delicious creamy chocolate mousse

Prep: **15 MINS**

Mmmmmm delicious chocolate mousse and it is not hard to make either! Give it a go!

YOU WILL NEED:

125ML DOUBLE CREAM
125G DARK CHOCOLATE
2 MEDIUM FREE-RANGE EGGS

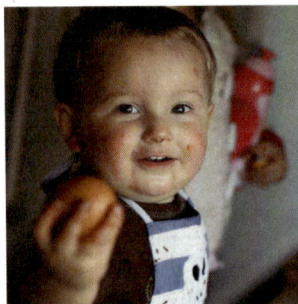

1. RIGHT, GRAB YOUR BIG PERSON AND LETS GO! HEAT THE CREAM UNTIL JUST BOILING. REMOVE IT FROM THE HEAT AND MELT THE CHOCOLATE IN A BOWL OVER A PAN OF BOILING WATER.

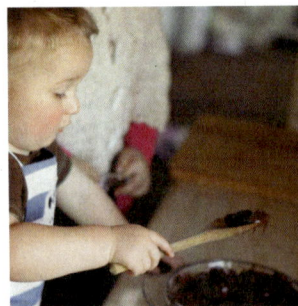

2. POUR THE MELTED CHOCOLATE INTO THE CREAM AND MIX CAREFULLY.

SEPARATE THE EGGS AND ADD THE YOLKS TO THE MIXTURE AND CAREFULLY STIR AGAIN.

3. WHILE THE BIG PEOPLE ARE DOING THIS BIT, GRAB ANOTHER BOWL AND ADD THE EGG WHITES TO IT.

GIVE THE EGG WHITES A GOOD WHISK, I WOULD USE AN ELECTRIC WHISK IF I WAS YOU!

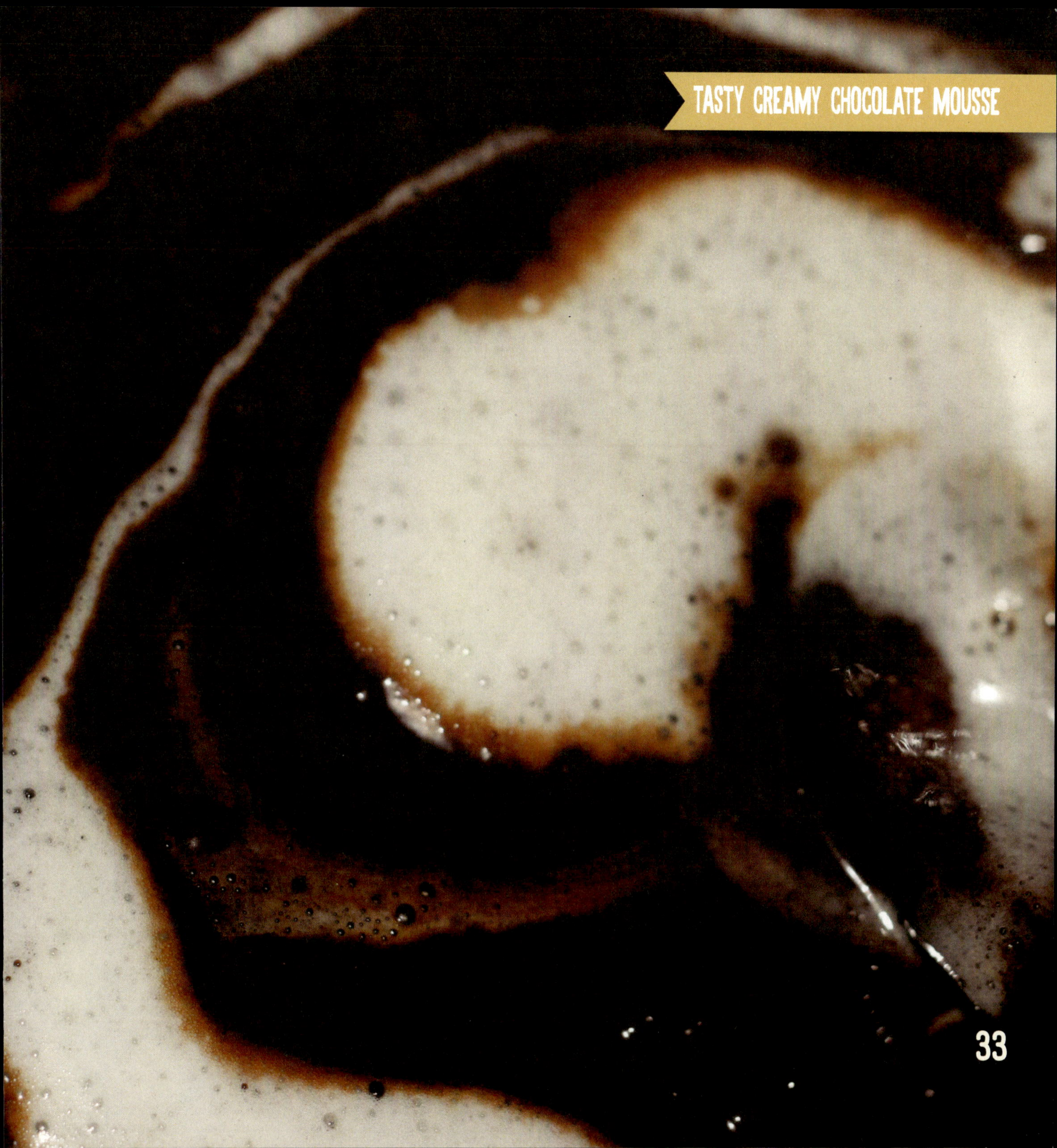

4. THE WHITES OF THE EGGS NEED TO BE WHISKED UNTIL THEY ARE STARTING TO GO STIFF. THEN CAREFULLY ADD THEM TO THE CHOCOLATE MIXTURE.

FOLD THE TWO MIXTURES TOGETHER BEING CAREFUL NOT TO LOSE TOO MUCH OF THE AIR AS THIS WILL MAKE YOUR MOUSSE LESS FLUFFY!

5. ONCE YOU ARE HAPPY WITH THE MOUSSE POUR IT INTO SMALL GLASSES OR BOWLS – WHAT EVER YOU WANT TO SERVE IT IN.

THESE CAN NOW BE PUT IN THE FRIDGE TO SET FOR AT LEAST 2 HOURS.

AFTER THIS TIME THEY CAN BE REMOVED AND SERVED WITH A DOLLOP OF FRESH WHIPPED CREAM AND A WAFER!

NOW DON'T FORGET, THERE WILL BE A BIG BOWL AND SPOON THAT WILL NEED LICKING, THIS SHOULD HELP PASS THE TIME WHILE WAITING FOR THE MOUSSES TO SET! NOM NOM NOM

MUMMY'S HOMEMADE QUICHE

This is Daddy's all time favourite lunch!

Prep: **30 MINS**
Cooking: **30-60 MINS**

This recipe really is one of our favourites! It is easy to make, quick and uses ingredients found in almost any kitchen! Try it as a snack, for lunch or maybe as part of a party platter. The other great thing about quiches is that you can fill them with whatever you like!

YOU WILL NEED:

FOR THE PASTRY:

175G PLAIN FLOUR
75G BUTTER
A FEW DROPS OF WARM WATER

FOR THE FILLING:

250G CHEDDAR CHEESE
RED AND GREEN PEPPERS
A FEW TOMATOES
200G BACON
5 FREE-RANGE EGGS
250ML MILK
SEASONING

1. FIRST OF ALL YOU NEED TO MAKE SOME PASTRY. TO DO THIS YOU NEED TO SIFT THE FLOUR WITH A PINCH OF SALT. THEN RUB THE BUTTER INTO IT TO MAKE BREADCRUMBS. YOU WILL NEED A PRETTY BIG BOWL FOR THIS.

2. NOW ADD A FEW DROPS OF WATER TO MAKE THE BREADCRUMBS TURN INTO A FIRM DOUGH. IT IS BEST TO LET IT REST FOR HALF HOUR NOW. YOUR ARMS COULD PROBABLY DO WITH A REST TOO!

3. ONCE YOU AND THE LAZY DOUGH ARE REFRESHED, YOU NEED TO ROLL IT OUT ONTO A LIGHTLY FLOURED SURFACE. THEN CUT IT INTO A HUGE CIRCLE BIG ENOUGH TO LINE YOUR FLAN DISH. I KNOW IT SOUNDS STUPID — AS WE ARE NOT MAKING FLAN!

4. NOW GET A BIG PERSON TO PREHEAT THE OVEN TO 190°C WHILST YOU WONDER WHAT A FLAN ACTUALLY IS.

5. POP THE 'FLAN' DISH IN THE OVEN FOR 20 MINS. ONCE IT HAS CRISPED UP A BIT TAKE IT OUT AND ASK THE VACANT LOOKING BIG PERSON TO REDUCE THE OVEN TEMPERATURE TO ABOUT 160°C.

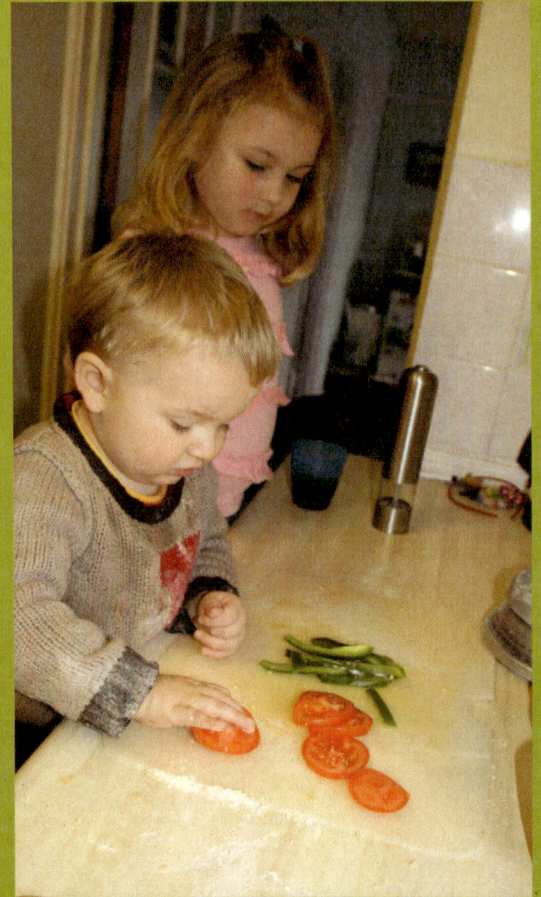

6. SPRINKLE THE DELICIOUS CHEESE INTO THE PASTRY BASE AND ADD SOME SLICES OF TOMATO AND PEPPERS.
NOW IS A GOOD TIME TO GET THE BIG PERSON TO FRY OFF THE BACON UNTIL CRISP SO WE CAN ADD IT TO OUR BASE.

7. COMBINE THE FINE FRESH FREE-RANGE EGGS WITH THE MILK IN A BIG BOWL AND SEASON IT WELL.

8. POUR THE EGGY-MILK MIXTURE OVER THE CHEESY BACON, TOMATO AND PEPPERS AND FILL UP YOUR PASTRY BASE. COOK IN THE OVEN FOR 30-40 MINS OR UNTIL IT IS SET.

ONCE IT IS DONE LET IT COOL FOR A BIT AND ENJOY!

REMEMBER YOU CAN USE ANY INGREDIENT IN THE BASE. SO IF YOU DON'T FANCY MEAT WHY NOT TRY TOMATOES, PEPPERS AND ONION?

IF HOWEVER YOU ARE A MEAT MONSTER THEN POP SOME BACON, HAM OR EVEN SAUSAGE IN YOUR QUICHE!

CAKE POPS

Soft sponge cake balls covered in melted chocolate on sticks!

Prep: **20 MINS**
Cooking: **15 MINS**

Cake pops are fun! They are great for parties and birthdays especially as you can make them any colour you like on the inside as well as any colour you like on the outside! Just add a few drops of food colouring to either the cake mix or to the melted white chocolate.

YOU WILL NEED:

FOR THE CAKE:
200G CASTER SUGAR
200G BUTTER
200G SELF RAISING FLOUR
3 FREE RANGE EGGS
1 TEASPOON BAKING POWDER
A FEW DROPS OF VANILLA EXTRACT

FOR THE POPS:
A SILICONE CAKE POP MOULD
A HANDFUL OF WOODEN OR PLASTIC LOLLIPOP STICKS
A FEW BARS OF YOUR FAVOURITE CHOCOLATE
SPRINKLES TO DECORATE

1. THERE ARE MANY METHODS OF MAKING CAKE POPS AND WE HAVE TRIED A FEW OF THEM. THE BEST WAY WE FOUND WAS TO USE A SILICONE CAKE POP MOULD. THESE ARE AVAILABLE AT MOST COOKERY SHOPS AND ARE NOT EXPENSIVE.

2. RIGHT SO FIRST OFF, BAKE A CAKE! ANY SIMPLE SPONGE CAKE WILL DO FINE. YOU CAN EVEN COLOUR THE SPONGE TO MAKE YOUR CAKE POPS MORE COLOURFUL.

SO BASICALLY MIX TOGETHER THE BUTTER, SELF RASING FLOUR, SUGAR AND THE EGGS AND BEAT IT UNTIL IT IS NICE AND SMOOTH. THEN ADD A FEW DROPS OF VANILLA EXTRACT AND A TEASPOON OF BAKING POWDER.

3. NOW SPOON THE MIXTURE INTO THE BOTTOM LAYER OF THE CAKE MOULD. SLIGHTLY OVERFILL THE DOMES AND POP THE OTHER HALF OF THE MOULD ON TOP

41

4. ASK YOUR BIG PERSON TO POP THE CAKE MOULD INTO A PRE-HEATED OVEN. ABOUT 180°C WILL BE FINE. NOW DUE TO THE SMALL SIZE OF THE LITTLE CAKE BALLS THEY WILL NOT NEED LONG IN THE OVEN. 10-15 MINUTES WILL BE FINE.

5. NOW ASK A BIG PERSON TO MELT THE CHOCOLATE IN A BOWL OVER A BOILING PAN OF WATER UNTIL IT IS NICE AND RUNNY.

NOW DIP THE END OF A STICK IN THE CHOCOLATE AND PUSH IT INTO ONE OF THE CAKE BALLS. THIS WILL HELP IT STICK. THEN DUNK THE CAKE BALL INTO THE CHOCOLATE AND COMPLETELY COVER IT.

6. NOW YOU CAN ADD THE DECORATIONS. ANYTHING YOU LIKE, SMALL SWEETS AND HUNDREDS AND THOUSANDS ARE QUITE GOOD.

NOW LET THEM COOL AND DRY. WE POPPED OURS IN THE FREEZER FOR 10 MINUTES TO GET THE CHOCOLATE TO GO ALL HARD AND COOL.

YOU CAN TRY VARIATIONS OF THIS RECIPE, LIKE USING WHITE CHOCOLATE OR WHITE CHOCOLATE MIXED WITH FOOD COLOURING TO REALLY MAKE YOUR LITTLE POPS STAND OUT!

SUMMER

Some great recipes to help you enjoy the great British summer!

EVERYONE LOVES SUMMERTIME!

IT'S THE TIME WHEN THE SUMMER FAYRES AND VILLAGE FETES HAPPEN AND NOT FORGETTING THE ALL IMPORTANT BRITISH BBQ! DON'T WORRY THOUGH, WE HAVE A RECIPE FOR HOMEMADE BURGERS IN THIS SECTION THAT ARE TRULY DELICIOUS!

EVERYTHING AND EVERYONE COMES TO LIFE DURING THESE SUNNIER MONTHS OF THE YEAR SO MAKE SURE YOU ENJOY THE GREAT OUTDOORS BUT DON'T FORGET THAT THERE ARE SOME GREAT SUMMER DISHES TO BE MADE IN THE KITCHEN TOO.

HAVE A LOOK THROUGH THIS SELECTION OF FUN DISHES THAT COMPLIMENT THE GREAT BRITISH SUMMER.

- A JUBILICIOUS ETON MESS
- GOAT'S CHEESE & BEETROOT SALAD
- MUMMY'S CHERRY CORDIAL
- SPANISH OMELETTE
- TEENY WEENY CHEESECAKES
- HOMEMADE BURGERS
- MIA'S STRAWBERRY JAM
- HOMEMADE LEMONADE

A JUBILICIOUS ETON MESS

A colourful, messy delight that is fit for royalty

This is a colourful twist on a classic British dessert. It can be made with left over home made meringue or broken up ready made meringues.

YOU WILL NEED:

BROKEN PIECES OF MERINGUE
500G FRESH STRAWBERRIES
300G FRESH BLUEBERRIES
400ML DOUBLE CREAM
1 TBSPN CASTER SUGAR

1. RIGHT THIS BIT IS GREAT FUN. SMASH ALL THE MERINGUE UP INTO CHUNKS IN A BOWL.

NOW CAREFULLY CUT UP THE STRAWBERRIES AND WASH THEM ALONG WITH THE BLUEBERRIES. POP THEM ALL TO ONE SIDE FOR NOW.

2. NOW IT'S TIME TO PUT YOUR ARMS TO WORK AND WHIP THE CREAM AND CASTOR SUGAR UNTIL IT FORMS LITTLE MOUNTAINS.

3. ONCE THE CREAM IS READY SPOON IT INTO THE BOWL WITH THE MERINGUE AND GENTLY MIX THEM ABOUT A LITTLE BIT.

47

4. NOW ADD SOME OF STRAWBERRIES AND BLUEBERRIES AND GIVE IT ANOTHER LITTLE MIX.

ADD THE REST OF THE FRUIT AND ARRANGE THEM HOW YOU LIKE. AS WE WERE PLANNING A UNION JACK THEME WE ROUGHLY SCATTERED THEM IN SECTIONS TO MATCH OUR GREAT FLAG.

5. CONTINUING WITH THIS THEME WE MASHED UP SOME OF THE STRAWBERRIES TO CREATE A SWEET RED SAUCE AND DRIBBLED THIS TO CREATE A CROSS.

THAT'S IT, ITS READY SO YOU CAN EITHER POP IT IN THE FRIDGE OR ENJOY STRAIGHT AWAY!

A JUBILICIOUS ETON MESS

FULL OF FRESHNESS!

GOAT'S CHEESE & BEETROOT SALAD

Prep: **15 MINS**
Cooking: **40 MINS**

A tasty salad with fresh goat's cheese and roasted beetroot

Now we all know that salad is not a child's most favouritist meal in the world and I don't care what you say! It isn't! But this little salad is actually very tasty and is pretty good for you! It is important to eat fresh vegetables so why not add some flavour to them!

YOU WILL NEED:

4 FRESH UNCOOKED BEETROOTS
A BUNCH OF FRESH ROCKET
A HANDFUL OF WALNUTS
2 SOFT ROUNDS OF GOATS CHEESE
A GLUG OF BALSAMIC GLAZE
A PINCH OF ROSEMARY

1. START OFF BY ASKING YOUR BIG PERSON TO BOIL THE FRESH SCRUBBED BEETROOT IN A PAN OF WATER FOR 30 MINUTES. DRAIN AND PUT IN A ROASTING TIN WITH A SPRINKLE OF ROSEMARY AND ROAST FOR 10 MINUTES.

2. WHILE THE BEETROOTS ARE ROASTING, WASH SOME FRESH ROCKET AND SMASH UP SOME WALNUTS!

3. WHEN THE BEETROOTS ARE DONE, REMOVE FROM THE OVEN AND REPLACE WITH THE SLICED RINGS OF GOAT'S CHEESE. HEAT THESE FOR A COUPLE OF MINUTES.

4. DICE ALL THE BEETROOT AND SPRINKLE ON TOP OF THE ROCKET ALONG WITH SOME WALNUTS, A DRIZZLE OF THE BALSAMIC GLAZE AND LASTLY THE SLIGHTLY MELTING GOAT'S CHEESE. DELICIOUS!

MUMMY'S CHERRY CORDIAL

A refreshingly simple cherry cordial

Prep: **15 MINS**
Cooking: **15 MINS**

This recipe is another quick and easy one that creates a delicious result that can be enjoyed for weeks to come. What's great is that the cherries can be substituted with other fruits throughout the year.

YOU WILL NEED:

500G FRESH CHERRIES
250G SUGAR
250ML WATER

IF YOU HAVE SPARE CHERRIES THEY CAN ALWAYS BE FROZEN FOR A LATER DATE.

1. THE CHERRIES NEED TO HAVE THEIR STONES REMOVED AND WILL NEED A GOOD WASH.

2. THEN THEY ARE READY TO BE ADDED TO A PRESERVING PAN ALONG WITH THE SUGAR AND WATER.
THIS NEEDS TO BE HEATED UNTIL THE SUGAR DISSOLVES AND THE CHERRIES ARE SOFT.

3. THEN THE MIXTURE CAN BE POURED INTO A BLENDER. WHIZ IT FOR A FEW SECONDS UNTIL SMOOTH.

WE THEN STRAINED THE CORDIAL THROUGH MUSLIN TO MAKE SURE IT IS LOVELY AND CLEAR. IT NEEDED A BIT OF PRESSING AT THE END BUT THE RESULT IS A FANTASTIC CLEAR CORDIAL THAT IS ALIVE WITH THE TASTE OF THE CHERRIES.

WE BOTTLED OURS USING STERILISED SCREW TOP BOTTLES SO WE CAN STORE THE CORDIAL AND ENJOY ALL YEAR ROUND. TO SERVE WE EITHER ADDED STILL OR SPARKLING WATER AND ICE.

ARCHER'S
·· SPECIAL ··
CHERRY
CORDIAL
★ ★ ★
50ML

ARCHER'S
·· SPECIAL ··
CHERRY
CORDIAL
★ ★ ★
50ML

SPANISH OMELETTE

A quick and easy, yet tasty lunch!

Prep: **15 MINS**
Cooking: **15 MINS**

This is a classic spanish recipe that is not only delicious and easy to make but also a lot of fun too!

YOU WILL NEED:

6 FREE RANGE EGGS
500G NEW POTATOES
1 ONION
A PINCH OF CHOPPED UP PARSLEY
SALT AND PEPPER

1. RIGHT FIRST OF ALL BREAK ALL OF THE EGGS INTO A LARGE BOWL AND GIVE THEM A GOOD MIX.

2. POP THE BOWL TO ONE SIDE SO WE CAN CUT UP ALL OF THE POTATOES INTO FAT LITTLE CHUNKS. ALSO CUT UP THE ONION INTO SMALL PIECES TOO.
GLUG A FEW DROPS OF OLIVE OIL INTO A FRYING PAN AND ADD THE POTATOES AND ONIONS. GENTLY FRY THEM FOR ABOUT 20 MINUTES UNTIL SOFT.

3. STRAIN THE POTATOES AND ONIONS THEN ADD THE BEATEN EGGS TO THE PAN AND FRY UNTIL THE EGGS ARE FIRM. ADD PLENTY OF SALT AND PEPPER AND THE PARSLEY.
NOW SLIDE THE OMELETTE OUT ONTO A PLATE THEN FLIP IT BACK INTO THE PAN AND COOK FOR A FURTHER FEW MINUTES

LET THE OMELETTE COOL FOR A FEW MINUTES THEN ITS TIME TO EAT!

55

FUND RAISING IDEAS & LOCAL SUPPORT

Fund raising ideas suitable for the whole family

We try and get involved in and support our local community as much as possible. We have also been lucky enough to get involved with some great fund raisers. If you would like to do the same then have a look at some of the things we got involved with last year.

FARM SHOPS AND VILLAGE FETES

THE FIRST EVER EVENT WE WERE INVITED TO ATTEND WAS AT OUR LOCAL FARM SHOP. THEY HOLD MANY ANNUAL EVENTS INCLUDING SMALL FOOD FESTIVALS. WE ATTENDED WITH A SMALL STALL SELLING HOMEMADE CAKES AND LEMONADE AND GIVING OUT INFORMATION ABOUT STROKE. OUR LOCAL STROKE ASSOCIATION OFFICE WERE KIND ENOUGH TO LEND US LOTS OF PROMOTIONAL MATERIAL AND FLYERS TO GIVE OUT ALONG WITH SOME VERY HANDY CHARITY SHAKERS.

CHARITIES ARE ALWAYS VERY HELPFUL SO IF YOU ARE THINKING OF DOING SOMETHING SIMILAR TO THIS THEN WHY NOT ASK YOUR CHOSEN CHARITY FOR ANY INFORMATION THAT YOU CAN HAND OUT?

LARGER EVENTS

SIZE DOESN'T MATTER BUT IF YOU WANT TO GO BIG THEN GO FOR IT! WE ATTENDED A FEW LARGE EVENTS WHILST PROMOTING THE FIRST BOOK AND HAD A GREAT TIME AT THEM ALL. OUR LOCAL HOSPITAL SET UP AN 'IT'S A KNOCKOUT' COMPETITION AND FETE TO RAISE FUNDS FOR THE HOSPITAL. THIS WENT DOWN EXTREMELY WELL AND WE WERE LUCKY ENOUGH TO HAVE A GLORIOUSLY SUNNY WEEKEND IN JUNE FOR IT!
DON'T FORGET THAT THESE LARGE EVENTS ARE MADE UP OF LOTS OF SMALL CONTRIBUTORS SO IF YOU WANT TO GET INVOLVED, DO SO. ALL CONTRIBUTIONS LARGE OR SMALL ARE ALWAYS WELL RECEIVED.

ATTENDING AND SUPPORTING OTHER EVENTS

DON'T FEEL THAT YOU HAVE TO GO AND SET UP A CHARITABLE EVENT TO RIVAL GLASTONBURY! IF YOU DO NOT HAVE THE FREE TIME TO COMMIT TO SETTING UP AND HELPING WITH AN EVENT THEN WHY NOT JUST ATTEND ONE THAT OTHER PEOPLE HAVE SET UP.
LOCAL SHOWS AND FETES ARE NOT ONLY GREAT FUND RAISING EVENTS BUT ARE ALWAYS A LOT OF FUN FOR THE PUBLIC.
FACE PAINTING IS A PARTICULAR FAVOURITE OF MINE!

VILLAGE BOAT RACES!

BOAT RACES ARE ANOTHER GREAT WAY OF RAISING MONEY FOR GOOD CAUSES AND THEY ARE ALSO A LOT OF FUN TOO!! THE BASIC RULES ARE THAT YOU HAVE TO MAKE YOUR OWN BOAT OR RAFT, BE ABLE TO GET IT TO THE RIVER THEN RACE AGAINST LOTS OF OTHER FUN SEEKING BOAT MAKERS TO THE FINISH LINE!
THESE ARE COMMON IN LOTS OF VILLAGES THROUGHOUT THE SUMMER, SO WHY NOT START ONE. PEOPLE CAN SPONSOR THE BOATS, PLACE BETS ON THE WINNER OR WHY NOT TIE IT IN WITH A VILLAGE FETE?

MY GRANDAD LED THIS FINE BOAT (NEARLY TO VICTORY) AND WE ALL HAD A GREAT LAUGH WATCHING THE RACE. BE WARNED THOUGH; YOU ARE LIKELY TO GET QUITE WET, EVEN IF YOU'RE NOT IN ONE OF THE BOATS!

TEENY WEENY CHEESECAKES

Mummy and Nanny's delicious little white chocolate cheesecakes

Prep: 25 MINS

This delicious family recipe is very versatile, it doesn't take long to make, doesn't need any cooking and you can add anything you like to the top. Fresh fruit works well.

YOU WILL NEED:

FOR THE BISCUIT BASE
500G CHOCOLATE CHIP COOKIES
50G BUTTER

FOR THE FILLING
250G MASCARPONE CHEESE
300G CREAM CHEESE
400G MELTED WHITE CHOCOLATE
300ML DOUBLE CREAM

1. THIS CHEESECAKE DOESN'T NEED COOKING SO WE DON'T NEED THE BIG PEOPLE MUCH!

SO LET'S START BY BASHING UP ALL THE BISCUITS IN A LARGE BOWL. OH HANG ON. WE DO NEED A BIG PERSON. GRAB ONE AND ASK THEM TO MELT THE BUTTER AND ADD IT TO YOUR BOWL.

2. GREASE SOME SMALL TINS WITH SOME OF THE BUTTER AND PLACE THEM ONTO A BAKING TRAY AND POUR THE BISCUIT MIXTURE INTO IT.

PRESS THE MIXTURE DOWN ESPECIALLY AROUND THE EDGES TO FORM THE BASE. WHEN THIS IS DONE THE BASES CAN BE CHILLING IN THE FRIDGE WHILE WE MAKE THE FILLING.

3. WHILE THAT BIG PERSON IS LOITERING ABOUT ASK THEM TO MELT THE WHITE CHOCOLATE IN A BOWL OVER A PAN OF BOILING WATER.

MIX THE CREAM CHEESE AND MASCARPONE TOGETHER AND ADD THE CREAM.

THEN ADD THE MELTED CHOCOLATE TO THE MIXTURE. BE A BIT CAREFUL HERE AS YOU CAN OVER MIX IT WHICH ISN'T GOOD, SO NICE AND SMOOTH WITH ALL THE INGREDIENTS COMBINED. HAVE A LITTLE TASTE AND SEE WHAT YOU THINK.

4. NOW SPOON THE FILLING INTO EACH OF THE BASE TINS EQUALLY. IF YOU ARE FEELING CREATIVE YOU CAN ADD A LITTLE SWIRL BY DROPPING A DRIP OF CHOCOLATE SAUCE ONTO THE FILLING AND MOVING IT WITH THE END OF A TEASPOON.

ONCE YOU HAVE FINISHED FIDDLING WITH THEM, POP THEM IN THE FRIDGE FOR A FEW HOURS.

5. WHEN YOU TAKE THEM OUT IT SOMETIMES HELPS TO USE A WARM CLOTH TO RUN AROUND THE TIN BEFORE REMOVING THEM.

61

BBQ READY HOMEMADE BURGERS

Prep: **30 MINS**
Cooking: **40 MINS**

Delicious homemade burgers ready for the BBQ!

Burgers are great especially when cooked on the BBQ. These home-made beauties are even better and can be made from any type of meat.

YOU WILL NEED:

540G MINCED BEEF
25G CHOPPED CORIANDER
1 RED ONION
1 TABLESPOON DIJON MUSTARD
1 FREE-RANGE EGG YOLK
1 SLICE OF CRUSTY BREAD
1 TABLESPOON OLIVE OIL
SALT & FRESHLY GROUND BLACK PEPPER

TO SERVE WE SUGGEST
A FRESH WHITE BAP
A HANDFUL OF FRESH LETTUCE
SOME HAND PICKED TOMATOES
A FEW SLICES OF CHEDDAR CHEESE &
A JUICY CORN ON THE COB

1. SO LETS START BY RIPPING THE BREAD UP TO CREATE BREADCRUMBS. YOU WANT REALLY SMALL LITTLE PIECES AND THE CRUSTIER THE BREAD THE BETTER!

2. NOW LETS HAVE A GO AT CHOPPING THE RED ONION. IF LIKE ME YOU ARE ONLY ALLOWED A PLASTIC KNIFE. THIS CAN BE QUITE DIFFICULT! SO AFTER A WHILE IT'S EASIER TO LET THE BIG PEOPLE FINISH THIS OFF.

3. NOW ADD ALL OF THE NON MEATY INGREDIENTS TO THE BOWL AND MIX IT ALL UP.

4. NOW ADD THE MINCE TO THE BOWL AND GIVE IT A GOOD STIR. AFTER A WHILE IT IS BETTER TO USE YOUR HANDS SO THAT YOU REALLY COMBINE ALL OF THE INGREDIENTS.

LIKE MANY OF THE RECIPES IN THIS BOOK, THERE IS A LOT OF ROOM TO ADAPT THE RECIPE TO SUIT YOUR OWN TASTE.

RATHER THAN BEEF YOU COULD USE PORK OR LAMB OR EVEN A VEGETARIAN ALTERNATIVE. YOU COULD ADD CHILLI PEPPERS IF YOU FANCY ADDING A BIT OF FIRE TO YOUR BURGERS BUT MAKE SURE YOU GET THE BIG PEOPLE TO TOUCH THE CHILIES!

LAMB AND SOME FRESH MINT WORKS WELL AS DOES PORK WITH SOME DICED APPLE! SO GET CREATIVE AND THINK UP SOME DELICIOUS BURGERS OF YOUR OWN!

5. RIGHT BACK TO THESE BURGERS. THE MIXTURE NEEDS TO BE QUITE STICKY SO IF IT STILL FALLS APART SLIGHTLY YOU CAN ALWAYS ADD ANOTHER EGG YOLK.

NOW YOU NEED TO SHAPE THE MIXTURE INTO BURGER SHAPES AND POP THEM IN THE FRIDGE FOR HALF AN HOUR. THEY SHOULD HOLD THEIR SHAPE AND BE READY TO COOK. IT IS A GOOD IDEA TO SEPARATE THE BURGERS WITH GREASE PROOF PAPER IF YOU ARE STACKING THEM AND ARE SHORT OF SPACE.

6. YOUR BURGERS ARE NOW READY TO COOK. IF THE WEATHER IS RUBBISH YOU CAN GRILL THEM FOR 15 MINUTES, TURNING THEM HALF WAY THROUGH OR IF MR SUN HAS COME OUT THEN GET THOSE BIG PEOPLE TO GET THE BBQ OUT AND GRILL THEM ON THERE FOR THAT DELICIOUS BBQ TASTE!

IF YOU HAVE A VEGETABLE GARDEN THEN PICK SOME FRESH TOMATOES AND LETTUCE TO ACCOMPANY YOUR BURGER IN A FRESH BAP ALONG WITH A SLICE OF MATURE CHEDDAR. DELICIOUS!

MIA'S STRAWBERRY JAM

Mia's first ever jam and still my favourite!

Prep: **30 MINS**
Cooking: **1 HOUR**

My big sister Mia has become quite the expert when it comes to making jam. This is how it all started, with her signature fresh strawberry jam.

YOU WILL NEED:

2KG FRESH BRITISH STRAWBERRIES
3 LEMONS (MAINLY FOR THE JUICE)
2KG JAM SUGAR
A KNOB OF BUTTER

1. WELL FIRST OF ALL YOU ARE GOING TO NEED A LOT OF STRAWBERRIES AND THE BEST WAY TO GET THESE IS TO GO PICK THEM YOURSELF!

THAT WAY YOU KNOW THEY ARE LOVELY AND FRESH AND IT'S A WHOLE LOT OF FUN PICKING THEM!

THERE ARE ALWAYS PICK-YOUR-OWN PLACES SCATTERED AROUND OUR GREAT BRITISH COUNTRYSIDE THIS WAY YOU KNOW EXACTLY WHERE THEY HAVE COME FROM AND YOU ARE SUPPORTING LOCAL FARMERS WHICH IS ALWAYS A GOOD THING TO DO!

2. NOW ADD THE STRAWBERRIES TO A PRESERVING PAN WITH THE SUGAR AND LEMON JUICE. YOU CAN SLICE A FEW BITS OF LEMON UP AND ADD THEM TOO. ASK YOUR BIG PERSON TO HEAT IT GENTLY TO DISSOLVE THE SUGAR.

DELICIOUS STRAWBERRIES!

3. WHILST THEY ARE DOING THIS, YOU CAN POP A PLATE CAREFULLY IN THE FREEZER. WE WILL NEED THIS LATER. WHILST YOU ARE THERE, WHY NOT TRY YOUR LUCK AND ASK FOR AN ICE POP, YOU NEVER KNOW, IT IS SUMMER!

4. ASK YOUR BIG HELPER TO TURN UP THE HEAT SO THAT THE MIXTURE BOILS FOR 4 MINUTES.

ONCE IT HAS BUBBLED AWAY FOR 4 MINUTES YOU NEED TO TEST IT. THIS IS EASY, YOU JUST NEED TO PLOP A SMALL TEASPOON FULL ONTO THE COLD PLATE AND AFTER A MINUTE OR SO, PUSH THE JAM WITH YOUR FINGER TO SEE IF IT IS SETTING. IF IT WRINKLES ON TOP THEN IT IS READY. IF IT IS NOT READY THEN RETURN TO THE BOIL FOR ANOTHER 2 MINUTES THEN REPEAT THE TEST.

5. ONCE DONE, YOU NEED TO GET CLEVER WITH YOUR BUTTER, THIS HELPS REMOVE THE SCUM. ADD A KNOB OF BUTTER TO THE MIXTURE. IF IT DOESN'T WORK THEN SPOON SOME OF THE SCUM OFF THE SURFACE.

6. LET THE JAM COOL FOR 15 MINUTES WHEN IT IS READY. GIVE IT A GENTLE STIR. ASK YOUR BIG HELPER TO HEAT THE OVEN TO 140°C AND STERILISE THE JAM JARS IN IT BY HEATING THEM FOR 30 MINUTES. ONCE THE JARS ARE READY THE JAM CAN BE POURED INTO THEM. LEAVE THIS TO THE BIG PEOPLE AND TELL THEM TO BE CAREFUL!

7. IMMEDIATELY COVER THE JAM WITH A WAXED DISC AND SEAL THE JARS.

8. THE JAM CAN BE STORED FOR LIKE 6 MONTHS IN A COOL, DRY PLACE.

WE USED SMALLER JAM JARS AS WE FOUND THAT HOMEMADE JAMS AND PRESERVES ARE FANTASTIC GIFTS FOR A SPECIAL OCCASIONS.

HOMEMADE LEMONADE

There's nothing more refreshing in the summer sun!

Fresh homemade lemonade is amazing on a sunny summer's day and it is not as hard to make as you may think. Give it a go and enjoy some age old refreshness!

YOU WILL NEED:

A BOWL FULL OF LEMONS (ABOUT 12).
300G SUGAR
4.5 PINTS OF BOILING WATER

1. FIRST OF ALL YOU WILL NEED TO SCRUB YOUR LEMONS! GIVE THEM A GOOD CLEAN AND POP THEM IN A LARGE BOWL. THEN ASK A BIG PERSON TO HELP REMOVE SOME OF THE ZEST FROM ABOUT HALF THE LEMONS. ALL OF THE WHITE BITS WILL NEED REMOVING AND DISCARDING.

2. NOW THIS BIT IS FUN – YOU NEED TO SQUEEZE ALL OF THE LEMON JUICE INTO A BOWL AND ADD THE LEMON ZEST. ADD THE SUGAR AND BOILING WATER AND GIVE IT A GOOD STIR. IT CAN NOW BE PUT INTO THE FRIDGE AND LEFT FOR A GOOD FEW HOURS IF NOT OVERNIGHT.

3. IN THE MORNING GIVE IT ANOTHER STIR AND TASTE. IT MAY NEED A TOUCH MORE SUGAR SO SEE WHAT YOU THINK. STRAIN IT THROUGH A SIEVE AND ITS READY. IT IS BEST TO SERVE MIXED WITH EITHER STILL OR IDEALLY SPARKLING WATER AND LOTS OF ICE. YUM!

THE MAKING OF OLIVER'S KITCHEN

The story of how we made the two books and the journey so far.....

After Oliver's stroke during that first year we were trying different activities with Ollie and Mia to keep ourselves busy. The worry and anxiety about Oliver reaching all the milestones that other children would reach was consuming us so we decided to do some cooking and involve the children.

Following that first dish we went on to cook many recipes and decided to share them online on a blog to keep family members up to date. Months later we were thinking of gift ideas for Ollie and Mia's great grandparents who at the time lived in France. Liz suggested that we create a book based on the recipes the kids had helped cook. From there the first book was born. We wrote, designed, photographed and printed the book ourselves and had so much fun creating it.

We launched Oliver's Kitchen (the book) at West Suffolk Hospital in 2011 at the official book launch. Apart from the original blog this was the first time the world would see Ollie's book and there were certainly enough people from the press present! It was quite a shock to us all as none of us had ever done any sort of interviews or photoshoots of this sort. We were talking to the BBC on the radio, to ITV on the television as well as having photographs taken to feature on the front pages of numerous newspapers.

We gave one of the recipes from the book to the hospital chef who cooked a huge batch of "star shaped cookies" for everyone which went down a treat! The coverage was fantastic and it really helped to launch the book in the eyes of the public.

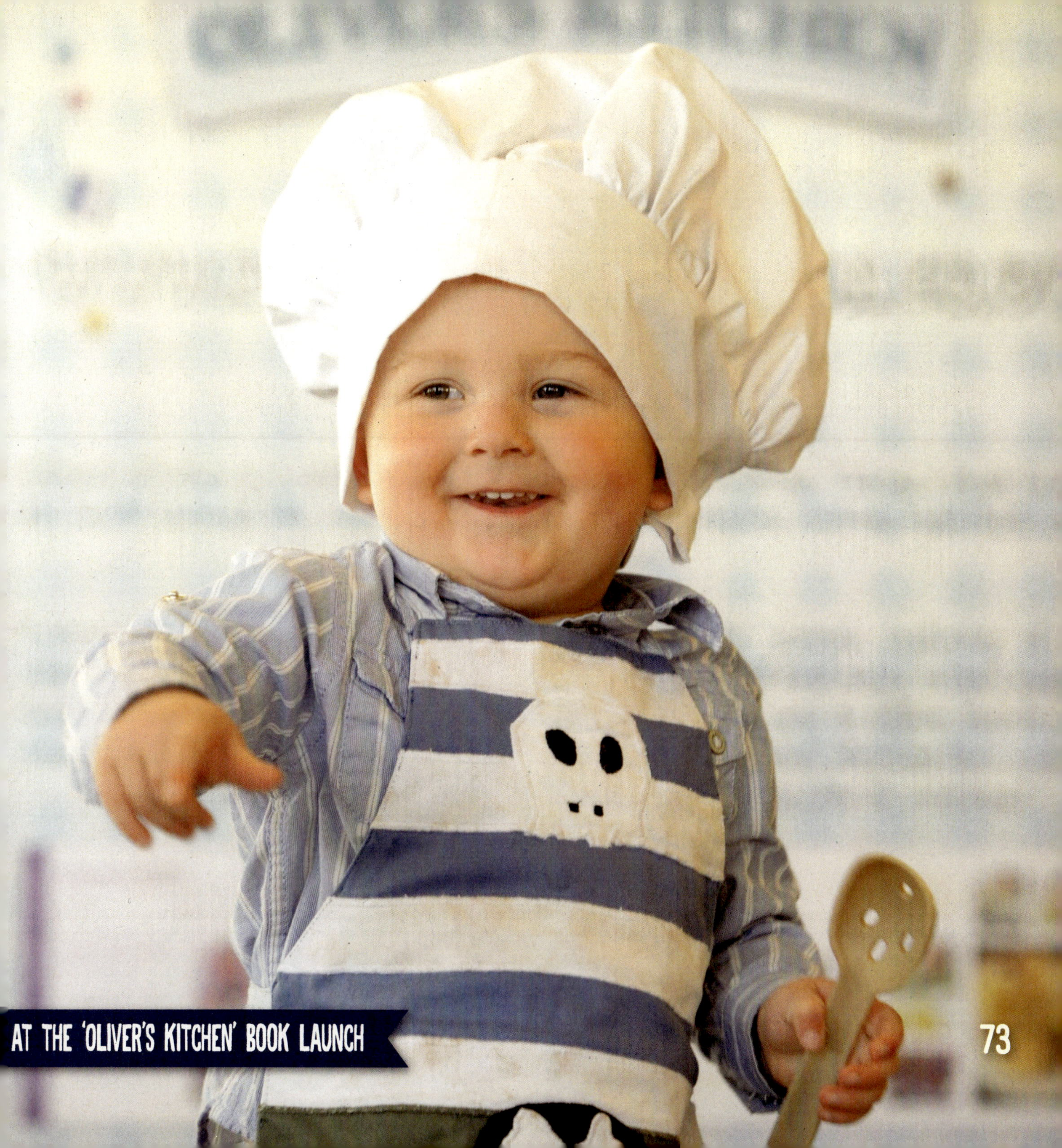

AT THE 'OLIVER'S KITCHEN' BOOK LAUNCH

TASTING THE HOSPITAL CHEF'S COOKIES!

OLIVER'S RECOVERY & PROGRESS

Oliver suffered a serious stroke whilst coming into this world. He was rushed to special care and spent over a week on the neonatal ward at West Suffolk Hospital.

He was eventually allowed home and we started the recovery process. Although we had seen scans of the damage inflicted on Ollie's brain, we had no idea as to the extent of what it could affect. So for the next year we watched his every move and tried everything we could to aid his recovery from physio to massage.

We waited for him to hit the 'normal' milestones that children reach and panicked if it was a day later than was to be expected.

We found cooking to be an excellent fun way of distracting ourselves from the worries of what the future might hold.

Ollie has recovered amazingly well and we feel truly blessed that he is how he is today! He shows no signs of the injury that his brain suffered and has met every milestone so far. We were told that Ollie's movement and coordination may be affected due to the part of the brain that was damaged but he was crawling, toddling, walking and running by the time he was two years old.

His speech is as it should be and he is a very bouncy, lively little boy that is always the first to bed and the first up in the morning waiting for another day to start! He has an amazing amount of 'fight' and determination which we are sure is why he has recovered the way he has. There is still a long way to go and we never know what may present itself around the next corner but we do feel incredibly lucky to be in the position we are in today.

Lots of others have unfortunately not been so lucky which is why we would love to raise the awareness of childhood strokes and make the support that is available much more accessible. When we were going though the early days we scoured the internet for a positive story of recovery and found very little to give us hope.

We know how valuable that word can be and if our story can offer another family an ounce of hope then we have achieved what we set out to do.

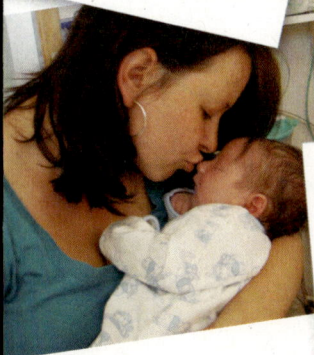

OLIVER'S KITCHEN IN THE NEWS

Following the launch of Oliver's Kitchen we found our little story popping up everywhere and whilst not taking any of it too seriously we enjoyed the coverage it was getting and consequently the money it was raising for the two benefitting charities.

We were asked to do interviews for local and national newspapers, we were heard talking about childhood strokes on the radio and seen on ITV news.

The book featured in the BBC Good Food magazine and had feature articles in magazines including the Suffolk magazine.

It has attracted the attention of celebrity chefs including Jamie Oliver who has so kindly written this book's foreword and supported us on twitter and instagram. We were even asked if we could help Professional

Master Chef runner up Ollie Boon cater for a very special birthday party!

It seems Ollie's story has touched the hearts of many as we started to receive emails and photographs from people around the world from Australia to New York, many of which stated how Oliver's ordeal has helped them cope with similar situations regarding stroke and even given them hope. This in itself has made the entire project so worthwhile for us as a family.

We were thrilled when we received a Highly Commended Certificate for the Life After Stroke Awards by the Stroke Association and feel very humbled by all of the well wishes we have received.

All of the coverage and support mentioned has helped us spread our message and we hope it can help make a difference.

AUTUMN

A beautiful time of year that is great for cooking

AUTUMN IS THE BEAUTIFUL BRONZE TIME OF YEAR WHERE EVERYTHING STARTS TO CHANGE AND GET READY FOR WINTER.

WITH OUR WEATHER SYSTEM AUTUMN IS ALWAYS A BIT UNPREDICTABLE BUT THERE ARE A FEW FANTASTIC EVENTS TO BE ENJOYED THIS TIME OF YEAR THAT MUST NOT BE FORGOTTEN. THINK SPOOKY FUN AT HALLOWEEN AND THE EXCITEMENT ON BONFIRE NIGHT WITH FIREWORKS AND SPARKLERS NOT TO MENTION THE ALL IMPORTANT HARVEST FESTIVAL!

TO COMPLIMENT THESE EXCITING TIMES, WE HAVE SOME GREAT RECIPES TO KEEP YOU GOING OUTSIDE AND WARM YOU UP FOR WHEN YOU COME INSIDE. TOFFEE APPLES AND FUDGE ARE FUN TREATS THAT ARE ALSO GREAT TO MAKE.

MAKE SURE YOU ENJOY THE GREAT OUTDOORS THIS AUTUMN AND ALL IT HAS TO OFFER.

- TOFFEE APPLES
- GRANNIE'S SPECIAL FUDGE
- TIRAMISU
- MIA'S GLITTER-PLUM JAM
- FRIDGE CAKE
- PINEAPPLE UPSIDE DOWN CAKE
- HOMEMADE PIZZA
- BANOFFEE PIE

HAVING FUN CAREFULLY PICKING THIS YEAR'S PUMPKIN

TOFFEE APPLES
Toffee covered apples on sticks!

Perfect at this time of year, especially fireworks night! These classic and tasty toffee covered apples are a treat not be forgotten.

YOU WILL NEED:

4-6 APPLES IF YOUR CHOICE
250G DEMERARA SUGAR
25G BUTTER
120ML WATER
HALF A TEASPOON OF VINEGAR
2 TABLESPOONS OF GOLDEN SYRUP
4-6 WOODEN SKEWERS

1. IT IS BEST TO LET A BIG PERSON DO THE HOT PART OF THIS RECIPE WHILE US LITTLE ONES CONCENTRATE ON THE FUN STUFF!

SO ASK YOUR BIG PERSON TO HEAT THE WATER OVER A MODERATE HEAT AND DISSOLVE THE SUGAR.

2. ONCE THE SUGAR HAS DISSOLVED THE GOLDEN SYRUP, BUTTER AND VINEGAR CAN BE STIRRED INTO IT.

WHEN ALL OF THIS HAS BEEN STIRRED A FEW TIMES IT NEEDS BOILING FOR ABOUT 10 MINUTES WITHOUT STIRRING.

3. WHEN THIS IS DONE A DROP SHOULD INSTANTLY TURN INTO A BALL IF DROPPED INTO COLD WATER. QUITE A FUN TEST!

81

4. WHILE THIS IS BEING DONE WE NEED TO SKEWER THE APPLES. WE NEED TO BE A BIT CAREFUL HERE BUT DON'T WORRY IF IT GETS A BIT TRICKY — YOU CAN DO THIS SOLDIER!

BASICALLY, PLACE THE APPLES ONTO A CHOPPING BOARD AND CAREFULLY PUSH THE WOODEN STICKS INTO THE CENTRE OF THEM SO THEY LOOK LIKE HUGE LOLLIPOPS!

5. WHEN THE TOFFEE IS READY IT IS TIME TO DIP THE APPLES. ANOTHER FUN PART!

WE WILL NEED THE BIG PEOPLE TO BRING THE HOT TOFFEE OVER AND TELL THEM TO NOT LET US TOUCH THE PAN, AS IT'S HOT! THIS WAY THEY FEEL IMPORTANT.

CAREFULLY DIP EACH APPLE INTO THE TOFFEE AND TWIZZLE IT AROUND SO THAT THE TOFFEE COVERS THE WHOLE APPLE.

6. THEN PLACE EACH APPLE ONTO A GREASED TRAY TO LET THE TOFFEE SET. THEY MAY NEED TO GO INTO THE FRIDGE. ONCE THEY ARE SET, THEY ARE READY TO ENJOY!

GRANNIE'S SPECIAL FUDGE

Prep: **30 MINS**
cooking: **40 MINS**

A great British classic, delicious creamy fudge

Great British fudge is fantastic and this recipe that I cooked here with my grannie is simply the best!

YOU WILL NEED:

410G EVAPORATED MILK
500G CASTER SUGAR
150G BUTTER
2 TEASPOONS VANILLA
EXTRACT

1. RIGHT, FIRST UP WE NEED TO LINE AN 18CM SQUARE CAKE TIN WITH GREASEPROOF PAPER. THEN POUR THE EVAPORATED MILK, SUGAR AND BUTTER INTO A HEAVY-BASED SAUCEPAN.

2. NOW ASK A BIG PERSON TO HEAT THE SAUCEPAN ON A LOW HEAT TO GENTLY MELT THE BUTTER AND DISSOLVE THE SUGAR. MAKE SURE THEY KEEP STIRRING IT!

3. ONCE THE SUGAR HAS DISSOLVED, THEY NEED TO BRING THE MIXTURE TO THE BOIL AND BOIL FOR ABOUT 20 MINUTES.

4. THE MIXTURE SHOULD BE A DELICIOUS LOOKING GOLDEN BROWN AND BE QUITE THICK BY NOW. IF YOU HAVE A SUGAR THERMOMETER THEN IT SHOULD BE ABOUT 115°C

5. IF YOU DON'T HAVE A THERMOMETER DON'T WORRY THERE IS ANOTHER TEST YOU CAN DO. COOK UNTIL THE MIXTURE IS GOLDEN BROWN AND THICKENED AND THEN DROP A LITTLE DROP INTO A GLASS OF COLD WATER. IF YOU CAN PICK THE COOLED DROP UP AND ROLL IT BETWEEN THUMB AND FOREFINGER IT IS FINE. ALLOW THE MIXTURE TO CONTINUE TO BOIL FOR ANOTHER FIVE TO TEN MINUTES, STIRRING ALL THE TIME.

6. ONCE IT IS DONE REMOVE IT FROM THE HEAT AND LET IT COOL FOR 5 MINUTES

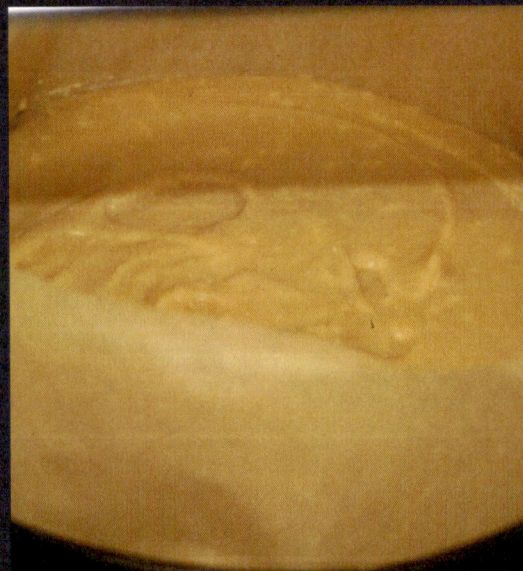

7. NOW BEAT THE MIXTURE IN THE PAN UNTIL IT STARTS TO THICKEN, LOOSES ITS GLOSS AND CHANGES TEXTURE FROM SMOOTH TO SLIGHTLY GRITTY. THEN ADD THE VANILLA AND STIR.

8. POUR THE MIXTURE INTO THE LINED CAKE TIN AND LEAVE IT TO SET. THIS COULD TAKE A GOOD FEW HOURS SO GO AND HAVE A PLAY AND COME BACK TO IT LATER.

9. WHEN IT IS SET, CAREFULLY CUT THE FUDGE INTO SMALL CUBES. THIS IS NOW READY TO BE ENJOYED!

A TASTY CREAMY TIRAMISU

A delicious creamy tiramisu that is a delight to make

Prep: **30 MINS**

Tiramisu. I have no idea what it means but it tastes delicious! There is no cooking involved so we hardly need the big people for this recipe but it's best to keep them around, they will only get bored on their own anyway.

YOU WILL NEED:

- 300ML OF DOUBLE CREAM
- 250G MASCARPONE
- 300ML CUSTARD
- 3 TSP COFFEE AND 300ML BOILING WATER
- 200G SPONGE FINGERS
- 4 TBSP GOLDEN CASTER SUGAR
- A SPLASH OF VANILLA
- A CHUNK OF CHOCOLATE AND A SPRINKLING OF COCOA POWDER

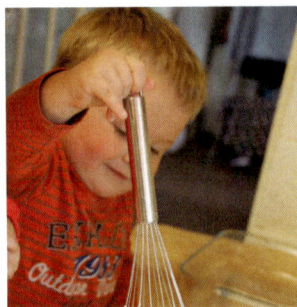

1. FIRST WE NEED TO MAKE SOME CUSTARDY MASCARPONE CREAM!

SO ADD 300ML OF DOUBLE CREAM AND 250G OF MASCARPONE TO 300ML OF CUSTARD AND GIVE IT A GOOD MIX IN THE BLENDER

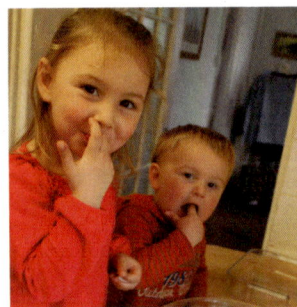

2. ADD 4 TABLESPOONS OF GOLDEN CASTER SUGAR AND A SPLASH OF VANILLA. WHEN THE MIXTURE IS LIKE THICK WHIPPED CREAM IT IS DONE.

THEN GET A BIG PERSON TO MAKE UP SOME COFFEE USING 3 TSP OF COFFEE AND 300ML OF BOILING WATER.

3. GET YOUR SERVING DISH READY AND START DIPPING SOME SPONGE FINGERS INTO THE COFFEE. MAKE SURE IT'S NOT HOT THOUGH!

4. PUT THE FINGERS INTO THE DISH THEN COVER WITH A LAYER OF CREAM MIXTURE. DO THIS AGAIN ALSO ADDING SOME GRATED CHOCOLATE.

FINISH WITH A LAYER OF CREAM AND TOP WITH SOME COCOA POWDER AND MORE GRATED CHOCOLATE.

POP IT IN THE FRIDGE FOR A FEW HOURS AND ITS ALL READY TO EAT!

YOU CAN SERVE THE TIRAMISU IN A NUMBER OF WAYS. WE DECIDED TO PLOP OURS INTO WINE GLASSES TO SERVE AS WE WERE BEING A BIT POSH!

IT'S ALWAYS BEST TO HAVE A LITTLE TASTE

GLITTER PLUM JAM

Mia's beautiful glittery tasty plum jam

Prep: **30 MINS**
Cooking: **1 HOUR**

Made using local plums with some added sparkle in the form of edible glitter, this jam is not only delicious but a little bit magical too!

YOU WILL NEED:

1.5KG FRESH LOCAL PLUMS
350G BRAMLEY APPLES
2 ORANGES
800G CASTER SUGAR
JUICE FROM A COUPLE OF LEMONS
2 TSP EDIBLE GLITTER

1. PEEL THE APPLES AND ASK A BIG PERSON TO CHOP THEM UP. THEY THEN NEED TO GO INTO A PAN WITH 500ML OF WATER AND BE BOILED FOR 15 MINS.

2. WHILST THE APPLES ARE BOILING, ASK THE BIG PERSON TO CHOP UP ALL OF THE PLUMS AND REMOVE THE STONES.
WHILE THEY ARE DOING THAT, YOU COULD BE JUICING THE ORANGES. THIS BIT IS FUN!

3. ASK YOUR GROWN UP TO ADD IT ALL TO THE PAN ALONG WITH THE SUGAR AND CONTINUE TO COOK FOR ANOTHER 15 MINUTES. ADD THE LEMON JUICE AND COOK UNTIL IT REACHES A TEMPERATURE OF 104°C

4. WHILST THE MIXTURE IS COOKING YOUR BIG PERSON NEEDS TO REGULARLY STIR IT. IF USING A PRESERVING PAN IT SHOULD NOT STICK TO THE BOTTOM BUT IT IS STILL A GOOD IDEA TO KEEP STIRRING.
MAKE SURE YOU TELL YOUR BIG PERSON THAT THE MIXTURE IS LIKELY TO BUBBLE UP AND WILL BE VERY HOT!

5. STIR IN SOME ORANGE ZEST AND ADD THE EDIBLE GLITTER. THIS CAN BE REMOVED FROM THE HEAT.
A GOOD TEST TO SEE IF THE JAM IS DONE IS TO POP A PLATE IN THE FREEZER FOR 10 MINUTES THEN PLOP A SMALL DOLLOP OF JAM ONTO THE PLATE, IF THE JAM IS QUITE RIGID AND WOBBLES A BIT LIKE JELLY THEN IT IS DONE.

6. PLACE YOUR GLASS JAM JARS INTO THE OVEN FOR 40 MINUTES AT 140°C THEN SPOON YOUR JAM INTO EACH JAR, THEY WILL NEED TO BE SEALED STRAIGHT AWAY AND LEFT OVERNIGHT. AFTER THIS THOUGH THEY ARE READY TO ENJOY OR STORE AWAY.

FRIDGE CAKE

Prep: **30 MINS**

A tasty dessert that can be chopped up into little treats

A delicious chocolate fridge cake that gets cooked in the fridge. I think. Well kind of anyway.

YOU WILL NEED:

125G BUTTER
3 TABLESPOONS DRINKING CHOCOLATE
1 TABLESPOON GOLDEN SYRUP
A GOOD HANDFUL SULTANAS
250G DIGESTIVE BISCUITS

200G MILK CHOCOLATE

1. OK. SO FIRST OF ALL, LINE A SHALLOW CAKE TIN WITH GREASEPROOF PAPER AND POP IT TO ONE SIDE. WE WILL NEED THIS LATER.

2. NOW LETS GET TO BASHING UP THE BISCUITS! GIVE THEM A GOOD BATTERING BUT STOP BEFORE THEY GET TOO SMALL. THEY WANT TO BE LIKE LITTLE CHUNKS AS THIS WILL HELP MAKE THE FRIDGE CAKE CRISPY!

3. NOW ASK A BIG PERSON TO MELT THE BUTTER, SYRUP AND DRINKING CHOCOLATE IN A SAUCEPAN. MAKE SURE THEY DON'T BURN IT THOUGH AS IT WILL RUIN THE CAKE!

4. NOW ADD THE SULTANAS TO THE MIX AND POUR IT ALL INTO THE BOWL OF BROKEN BISCUITS. GIVE THEM A GOOD STIR. IT SHOULD BE QUITE STIFF AND NOT VERY RUNNY AT THIS STAGE. IF IT IS TOO RUNNY THEN YOU HAVE DONE SOMETHING WRONG. I DON'T KNOW WHAT YOU'VE DONE BUT IT'S POSSIBLY RUINED SO YOU MIGHT HAVE TO START AGAIN.

OR IT MIGHT BE FINE.

5. WHEN YOU HAVE GOT IT RIGHT YOU CAN POUR IT INTO THE BAKING TIN. NOW PRESS IT DOWN AND SPREAD IT SO THAT IT'S EVEN ALL OVER.

6. NOW ASK A BIG PERSON TO MELT THE CHOCOLATE AND POUR IT OVER THE CAKE AND SPREAD EVENLY.

POP THE CAKE INTO THE FRIDGE TO COOL FOR A FEW HOURS. THEN SLICE IT UP INTO CHUNKS AND ENJOY!

CHARITY SKYDIVE FOR STROKE

Our crazy team raising money for The Stroke Association

Prep: **2 MONTHS**
Falling: **6 MINS**

Daddy

As a way of raising money for The Stroke Association I decided that we should do a Charity Skydive. After looking into it I discovered that two year olds are too young to jump out of airplanes.

Rather disappointed, I got Daddy to do it instead! He organised it and recruited a team of willing volunteers. He found an airfield in Suffolk that offers Tandem Skydives, jumping from approximately 13,000 feet in the sky. Now that is high!

The first task was to see how many people he could get to agree to jump. Everyone was very excited by the idea and we soon had our team signed up. The team dispersed and spent 2 months collecting sponsorships for the jump.

As the jump got closer and closer everyone seemed to be concentrating more on the sponsorships than they were on the jump. That was great until they all realised that the day of the jump had snuck up on them and they were all terrified!

We headed down to the airfield and got the team kitted out in their flight gear. It was very exciting and despite their obvious fear, most of the jumpers looked pretty excited! We gave Daddy a hug, wished him luck and up they went! High, high up into the sky until the airplane was just a tiny dot.. Then after a while these even smaller dots appeared and all of sudden their parachutes popped out! Everyone landed safely and thoroughly enjoyed the experience.

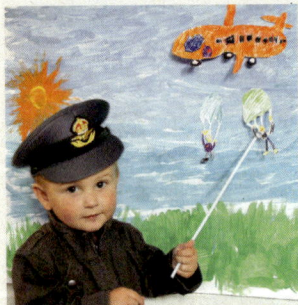

We raised over one thousand pounds for charity so it was well and truly, mission accomplished!!

PINEAPPLE UPSIDE DOWN CAKE

A ridiculously tasty cake, just a little backward!

Prep: **30 MINS**
Cooking: **40 MINS**

This is a very refreshing cake that is a lot of fun to make. You can add cherries as a decoration if you like or just enjoy it as it is! I think more cakes should be made upside down.

YOU WILL NEED:

FOR THE TOPPING:
50G SOFTENED BUTTER
50G LIGHT SOFT BROWN SUGAR
1 FRESH PINEAPPLE (OR PINEAPPLE RINGS)

FOR THE CAKE:
100G SOFTENED BUTTER
100G GOLDEN CASTER SUGAR
100G SELF-RAISING FLOUR
1 TSP BAKING POWDER
1 TSP VANILLA EXTRACT
2 FREE RANGE EGGS

1. FIRST OF ALL YOU NEED TO GET A BIG PERSON TO PREHEAT THE OVEN TO 180C SO THAT IT IS NICE AND HOT READY FOR WHEN WE NEED IT.

2. NOW WE NEED TO MAKE THE TOPPING. WE DO THIS FIRST REMEMBER BECAUSE FOR THIS CAKE WE ARE DOING EVERYTHING BACKWARDS OR UPSIDE DOWN! SO WE NEED TO BEAT THE SUGAR AND BUTTER TOGETHER UNTIL NICE AND CREAMY.

3. NOW WE NEED TO SPREAD THIS MIXTURE OVER THE BOTTOM AND SIDES OF A CAKE TIN. THEN ASK YOUR DESIGNATED BIG PERSON TO CAREFULLY SLICE UP THE PINEAPPLE READY FOR YOU TO ADD TO THE TIN.

4. NOW PLACE ALL OF THE CAKE INGREDIENTS INTO A BOWL AND MIX IT LIKE MAD! GO ON GIVE IT A GOOD OLD MIX! FASTER!

5. ONCE IT IS ALL MIXED OR YOU'RE TOO TIRED TO CARRY ON MIXING, POUR THE MIXTURE INTO THE CAKE TIN ALL OVER AND AROUND THE PINEAPPLE.

6. ASK YOUR BIG PERSON TO POP IT INTO THE OVEN FOR ABOUT 35 MINUTES. ONCE IT IS COOKED, LET IT STAND FOR 5 MINUTES THEN FLIP IT OUT ONTO A PLATE AND DUST WITH SOME ICING SUGAR.

NOW IT IS READY TO ENJOY!

WE MADE THIS ONE FOR AUNT SAM'S BIRTHDAY AND IT WAS YUMMY!

HELPING EACH OTHER IN THE KITCHEN WORKS A TREAT

HOMEMADE PIZZA

Everyone loves pizza, but it's so much better homemade!

Prep: **20 MINS**
Cooking: **10 MINS**

This recipe is great as you can make any pizza with any combination of toppings that you can think of. Here we show you the basics of making a pizza base.

YOU WILL NEED:

300G STRONG WHITE BREAD FLOUR
1 TEASPOON OF ACTIVE YEAST
A PINCH OF SALT
1 TABLESPOON OLIVE OIL

100ML PASSATTA
HANDFUL OF BASIL
1 CLOVE OF GARLIC, CRUSHED
1 TOMATO
A HANDFUL OF GRATED CHEESE

TOPPING – WHAT EVER YOU LIKE

1. PLACE THE FLOUR, YEAST AND SALT IN A BOWL AND MIX.

MAKE A LITTLE WELL AND POUR 200ML OF WARM WATER AND THE OLIVE OIL INTO IT. MIX IT UP WITH YOUR TRUSTY WOODEN SPOON TO FORM A DOUGH.

TURN IT OUT ONTO A FLOURED SURFACE THEN KNEED IT FOR ABOUT 5 MINUTES. THEN LEAVE IT TO ONE SIDE WHILE WE MAKE THE SAUCE.

2. THE SAUCE IS ALSO EASY. MIX THE PASSATTA WITH THE GARLIC AND CHOPPED BASIL. NOW IT IS JUST THE TOPPING!

3. ROLL OUT YOUR DOUGH AND FORM IT INTO A PIZZA SHAPE. TRANSFER TO A COOKING STONE AND SPREAD THE SAUCE EVENLY OVER THE DOUGH'S SURFACE.

ADD SOME SLICED TOMATOES AND GRATED CHEESE. WE NOW ADDED OUR OTHER TOPPINGS. WE USED MOZZARELLA AND TOMATO TO MAKE A MARGHERITA FOR ONE PIZZA. PEPPERONI AND HAM TO MAKE A MEATY FEAST ON ANOTHER. YOU CAN USE WHATEVER YOU LIKE.

4. PLACE THE STONE IN THE OVEN AND COOK THE PIZZA FOR ABOUT 10 MINS UNTIL CRISPY. ENJOY!

BANOFFEE PIE

Prep: **30 MINS**

It's a pie made from bananas and toffee, banoffee! Get it? Daddy didn't!

Mia makes a beautiful dessert and tries to explain to Daddy why it's called a banoffee pie.

YOU WILL NEED:

150G DIGESTIVE BISCUITS
3 LARGE BANANAS
75G BUTTER
250ML DOUBLE CREAM, WHIPPED
UNTIL IT FORMS SOFT PEAKS
A PINCH OF COCOA POWDER
GRATED CHOCOLATE

A TIN OF CREAM CARAMEL

1. RIGHT, HERE WE GO. LET'S BREAK UP ALL THE BISCUITS! GIVE THEM A GOOD BATTERING. PLACE THE BISCUITS AND 75G BUTTER INTO A BIG MIXING BOWL AND MIX THEM ALL UP!

2. THEN TIP THE MIXTURE INTO A DISH AND FIRMLY PUSH DOWN ESPECIALLY INTO THE CORNERS TO MAKE A COMPACT BASE.

3. THEN CHOP UP, THE BANANAS INTO SLICES AND MIX THEM UP WITH THE CARAMEL.

THIS MAKES UP THE BANOFFEE!

THIS CAN THEN BE POURED AND SPREAD OVER THE BUTTERY BISCUIT BASE. NOW POP IT IN THE FRIDGE TO COOL.

DELICIOUS BANOFFEE PIE

4. AFTER ABOUT 30 MINUTES, REMOVE THE PIE BASE FROM THE FRIDGE AND TOP WITH THE WHIPPED CREAM.

DROP A FEW EXTRA BITS OF BANANA ON THE TOP AND SPRINKLE WITH COCOA POWDER AND GRATED CHOCOLATE.

5. THIS IS AN INCREDIBLY EASY RECIPE THAT IS QUICK AND FUN BUT MOST OF ALL LOOKS AND TASTES AMAZING IN NO TIME! ENJOY.

WINTER

Here are some great heart warming recipes

OH BABY IT'S COLD OUTSIDE! BUT DON'T LET THAT GET YOU DOWN, WHEN IT'S COLD OUTSIDE ITS BEST TO ENJOY SOME HOMEMADE SOUP INSIDE!

THERE IS A WHOLE LOT OF FUN TO BE HAD AT WINTER TIME, FESTIVE PREPARATIONS, BUILDING SNOWMEN, SLEDGING, GETTING READY FOR A BRAND NEW YEAR AND THAT'S NOT TO MENTION THE FEASTS TO BE MADE IN THE KITCHEN! BUT MOST IMPORTANTLY IT'S CHRISTMAAAAAS TIME!!

IN THESE FOLLOWING PAGES WE MAKE SOME INCREDIBLE DISHES SUCH AS A WINTERY ROASTED ONION SOUP, A SURPRISINGLY HEALTHY JAM ROLY POLY AND SOME CHRISTMASSY CANDY CANE REINDEERS! SO GET AMONGST IT AND ENJOY WHAT I PERSONALLY THINK IS THE BEST TIME OF THE YEAR!

- WINTERY ROAST ONION SOUP
- JAM ROLY POLY
- MEXICAN EGGS
- CHOCOLATE BROWNIES
- RATATOUILLE
- CANDY CANE REINDEERS
- STICKY TOFFEE PUDDING
- REDCURRANT JELLY

WINTERY ROASTED ONION SOUP

The best thing to warm you up after some snowy fun!

Prep: 30 MINS
Cooking: 60 MINS

A delicious and healthy soup guaranteed to warm you up on even the coldest days! Ideally enjoy with some warm homemade bread.

YOU WILL NEED:

ABOUT 5 MEDIUM ONIONS

A COUPLE OF CLOVES OF GARLIC

1 LITRE VEGETABLE STOCK

A GLUG OF OLIVE OIL

1 TABLESPOON WHOLEGRAIN MUSTARD

A SPRINKLE OF FRESH PARSLEY

A TABLESPOON FULL OF THYME

1. WINTER TIME IS A GREAT TIME OF YEAR FOR SOUPS AND THIS RECIPE IS DELICIOUS. SO GRAB YOUR BIG PERSON AND ASK THEM TO PREHEAT THE OVEN TO 220°C.

THE ONIONS NEED PEELING AND SPRINKLING WITH SOME THYME THEN THEY ARE READY FOR THE OVEN FOR 40 MINS.

ADD THE GARLIC CLOVES FOR THE LAST 20 MINS.

2. ONCE THEY ARE NICE AND SOFT, ROUGHLY CHOP THE ONIONS. CRUSH THE GARLIC THEN POP THEM INTO A PAN WITH THE STOCK, MUSTARD AND PARSLEY AND SIMMER FOR 20 MINS.

ROASTING THE ONIONS FIRST GIVES A GREAT CARAMELISED TASTE

3. AFTER THE SOUP HAS SIMMERED IT IS REALLY UP TO YOU HOW YOU SERVE IT. YOU COULD LADLE IT STRAIGHT INTO BOWLS AS IT IS OR YOU CAN POUR IT INTO A BLENDER AND WHIZZ IT TO YOUR DESIRED CONSISTENCY.

WE HAVE TRIED BOTH WAYS AND THEY ARE EQUALLY DELICIOUS. IF YOU DO BLEND IT, THEN WHIZZ IT FOR SHORT PERIODS AT A TIME SO YOU DON'T OVER DO IT.

4. SOUP IS ALWAYS BEST ENJOYED WITH A FRESH CRUSTY ROLL!

A LIGHT JAM ROLY POLY

A fun jam roly poly made with Mia's special jam

Prep: **30 MINS**
Cooking: **40 MINS**

This fun recipe is not only tasty but it is not actually that naughty as it does not contain any butter. So you do not have to feel too guilty after eating it! I don't tend to feel particularly guilty after desserts but some do apparently!

YOU WILL NEED:

3 LARGE FREE RANGE EGGS
100G CASTER SUGAR
150G JAM — WE USED STRAWBERRY
1 TEASPOON VANILLA EXTRACT
115G PLAIN FLOUR

1. OK SO GRAB YOUR BIG PERSON AND ASK THEM TO PREHEAT THE OVEN TO 200°C.

WHILE THEY DO THAT WE NEED TO GREASE THE SIDES AND BASE OF A BAKING TIN. THEN LINE IT WITH GREASEPROOF PAPER.

2. NOW ADD THE EGGS, SUGAR AND VANILLA EXTRACT TO A BOWL AND MIX IT UP. NOW PASS THE BOWL TO A BIG PERSON AND ASK THEM TO HEAT IT OVER A PAN OF BOILING WATER AND WHISK IT WITH AN ELECTRIC WHISK.

WHILE THEY DO THIS WE CAN PRACTICE ROLY POLYS IN THE OTHER ROOM.

3. WHEN THE MIXTURE IS CREAMY AND THICK ASK THEM TO BRING IT BACK SO WE CAN MIX IT UP FOR ANOTHER 5 MINUTES.

4. SIFT OVER HALF OF THE FLOUR AND GENTLY FOLD IT INTO THE MIXTURE. ONCE IT IS MIXED IN, SIFT IN THE OTHER HALF OF THE FLOUR AND AGAIN, GENTLY FOLD IT INTO THE MIXTURE. THIS BIT IS QUITE IMPORTANT AS IT KEEPS THE AIR IN THE MIXTURE WHICH WILL HELP KEEP THE CAKE NICE AND FLUFFY AND LIGHT.

5. POUR THE MIXTURE INTO THE TIN AND SPREAD IT OUT EVENLY USING A SPATULA.

6. NOW IT CAN BE BAKED IN THE OVEN FOR ABOUT 10 MINUTES. BE CAREFUL NOT TO OVERCOOK THE CAKE AS IT MAKES IT MUCH MORE DIFFICULT TO ROLL. IT SHOULD BOUNCE BACK WHEN YOU PRESS THE MIDDLE GENTLY. DON'T JUMP ON IT AS IT IS NOT THAT BOUNCY!

7. LAY A DAMP TABLE CLOTH ONTO A SURFACE AND COVER WITH A PIECE OF GREASEPROOF PAPER. SPRINKLE A BIT OF SUGAR ONTO IT TO STOP THE CAKE STICKING TO IT.

8. NOW WHEN THE CAKE IS READY, TURN IT OUT ONTO THE PAPER. CAREFULLY TRIM THE EDGES OFF AND SCORE THE LENGTH OF ONE SIDE ABOUT 2CM IN FROM THE EDGE. THIS MAKES IT EASIER TO ROLL.

9. SPREAD THE JAM OVER THE WHOLE CAKE AND START ROLLING! KEEP IT TIGHT AND ROLL IT IN TO A NICE JAMMY LOG! TRY AND KEEP IT AS ROUND AS POSSIBLE THEN LEAVE IT TO COOL ON A WIRE RACK.

ADD A DUSTING OF ICING SUGAR TO GIVE IT THAT CHRISTMASSY LOOK!

123

BAKED MEXICAN EGGS

A delicious breakfast alternative that's easy too

Prep: **20 MINS**
Cooking: **10 MINS**

Now yours don't have to be Mexican, it depends on what ingredients you use! As with a lot of our recipes, it is easy to add or change your own ingredients. So grab your favourites and get ready for a tasty breakfast treat.

YOU WILL NEED:

A LARGE FREE-RANGE EGG
GREEN AND RED PEPPERS
TOMATOES
BACON
CHORIZO OR OTHER SAUSAGE
A SPRINKLE OF PARSLEY

1. IT IS BEST TO GET ALL YOUR INGREDIENTS READY FIRST SO GRAB ALL YOUR VEGETABLES AND SLICE THEM UP.
YOU WILL ALSO NEED SOME SMALL OVEN-PROOF DISHES FOR THESE SPECIAL EGGS. THEY ARE AVAILABLE AT MOST KITCHEN SHOPS SO DON'T WORRY.

2. NICELY ASK YOUR PREFERRED BIG PERSON TO PREHEAT THE OVEN FOR YOU.

WHILST THEY ARE AT IT THEY COULD PREPARE A FRYING PAN WITH A FEW DROPS OF OLIVE OIL OVER SOME HEAT TOO.

3. THE BACON, CHORIZO OR OTHER MEAT WILL NEED TO BE COOKED IN THE OIL BEFORE ADDING THE SLICED PEPPERS AND TOMATOES THAT YOU CLEVERLY PREPARED EARLIER. JUST SOFTEN THESE UP FOR A FEW MINUTES.

4. REMEMBER YOU CAN ADD ANYTHING YOU FANCY OR HAVE TO HAND, SO GIVE IT ALL TO YOUR BIG PERSON.

5. NOW ONCE YOU HAVE ALL YOUR INGREDIENTS READY YOU CAN SPRINKLE THEM INTO YOUR BAKING DISHES. YOU DO NOT WANT TO ADD TOO MUCH THOUGH BECAUSE REMEMBER, YOU NEED TO ADD AN EGG TO IT YET!

WE HAVE MADE LOTS OF VARIATIONS OF THIS DISH AND HAVE TRIED LOTS OF COMBINATIONS OF DIFFERENT FOODS. THIS IS HALF THE FUN SO MAKE SURE YOU FIND THE TIME TO EXPERIMENT!

6. NOW ONCE YOU HAVE DECIDED ON WHAT IS GOING INTO YOUR DISHES IT IS TIME TO CRACK AN EGG INTO IT!
THIS IS EASY, JUST SIMPLY CRACK AN EGG INTO THE DISH AND LET IT RUN BETWEEN ALL THE DIFFERENT LAYERS.

7. ASK YOUR BIG PERSON TO POP YOUR DISH INTO THE OVEN AND LET IT COOK FOR ANYWHERE BETWEEN 5 AND 10 MINUTES OR UNTIL THE EGG WHITE IS EXACTLY THAT, WHITE.

THE TIMING IS NOT TOO CRUCIAL ALTHOUGH TRY NOT TO OVER-COOK AS IT MAY STICK TO THE EDGES.

8. WHEN IT IS READY AND YOUR BIG PERSON HAS TAKEN IT OUT OF THE OVEN, LET IT COOL SLIGHTLY AS THE DISH WILL BE VERY HOT AND ENJOY!

OBVIOUSLY HALF THE FUN (IF NOT MORE) IS IN THE EATING SO TRY YOURS ON ITS OWN OR MAYBE WITH SOME TOAST.

NOM NOM NOM

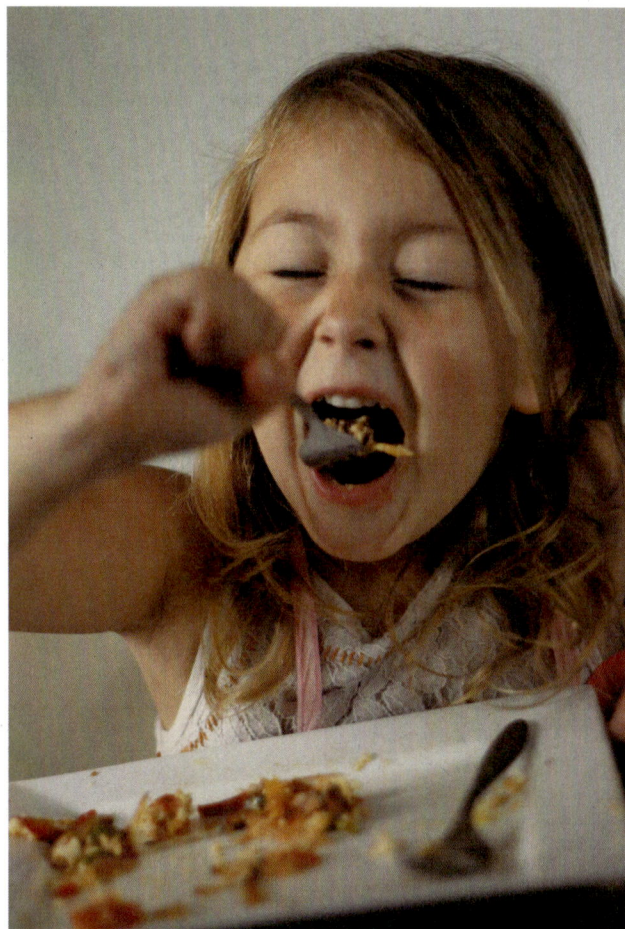

127

SERIOUSLY CHOCOLATEY BROWNIES

They're not funny brownies, they're seriously chocolatey!

Prep: **25 MINS**
Cooking: **25 MINS**

Brownies are funny actually, we don't know what they are! Are they crunchy? Are they soft? Are they dry? Are they moist? They are all of those things which is why we love them!

YOU WILL NEED:

250G UNSALTED BUTTER
200G DARK CHOCOLATE (70% COCOA)
80G COCOA POWDER
65G PLAIN FLOUR
1 TEASPOON BAKING POWDER
360G CASTER SUGAR
4 LARGE FREE-RANGE EGGS

1. RIGHT, GET YOUR BIG PERSON TO PREHEAT THE OVEN TO 180°C AND START LINING A BAKING TRAY WITH GREASEPROOF PAPER.

2. NOW WHILST YOU HAVE YOUR BIG PERSON'S ATTENTION, ASK THEM TO HEAT UP SOME WATER IN A SAUCEPAN AND POP A BOWL OVER IT. THEY THEN NEED TO ADD THE CHOCOLATE AND BUTTER. MAKE SURE THEY KEEP AND EYE ON IT THOUGH AND KEEP STIRRING IT. IT IS VERY EASY TO BURN THE CHOCOLATE IF YOU DO NOT STIR IT OFTEN ENOUGH.

3. WHILE THEY ARE DOING THIS BIT, YOU NEED TO GET A BIG BOWL OUT AND START ADDING THE OTHER INGREDIENTS. START WITH THE COCOA POWDER, THEN THE FLOUR AND THEN THE BAKING POWDER AND SUGAR. THIS WILL NEED STIRRING.

4. NOW ADD THE EGGS AND CHOCOLATE MIXTURE AND BEAT THE UNTIL IT IS ALL NICE AND SMOOTH. IT SHOULD LOOK QUITE SILKY.

5. IT IS NOW TIME FOR THE COOKING SO MAKE SURE YOU HAVE SOMEONE BIG ENOUGH NEAR BY TO POP YOUR BROWNIES IN THE OVEN FOR YOU.
SO, POUR THE BROWNIE MIXTURE IN A BAKING TIN AND LET IT SETTLE AS LEVEL AS POSSIBLE. NOW IT'S TIME FOR THE OVEN!

6. YOUR BROWNIES NEED TO COOK FOR ABOUT 25 MINUTES BUT KEEP AN EYE ON THEM AS IDEALLY YOU WANT THEM TO BE SLIGHTLY CRUNCHY ON THE OUTSIDE BUT SOFT AND GOOEY IN THE MIDDLE. REMEMBER THIS IF YOU TEST THEM WITH A KNIFE AS YOU DO NOT WANT THE KNIFE TO COME OUT COMPLETELY CLEAN LIKE WITH NORMAL CAKES AS THIS WOULD MEAN THE BROWNIES ARE OVER COOKED!

7. ONCE THEY ARE COOKED ABSOLUTELY PERFECTLY ALLOW THEM TO COOL FOR A FEW MINUTES THEN ENJOY WITH A DOLLOP OF CREAM OR ICE CREAM.

RATATOUILLE

You've all seen the film, now taste this delicious recipe

Prep/cooking: **50 MINS**

Vegetables are great and this recipe uses loads of them! Just take a look at all the lovely, bright colours and shapes then follow this recipe to make a truly delicious, colourful, healthy meal!

YOU WILL NEED:

- 2 AUBERGINES
- 3 COURGETTES
- 2 RED ONIONS
- 1 RED AND 1 GREEN PEPPER
- 2 LARGE TOMATOES
- A SMALL HANDFUL OF BASIL
- 3 TSP OLIVE OIL
- 3 GARLIC CLOVES
- 1 TBSP RED WINE VINEGAR

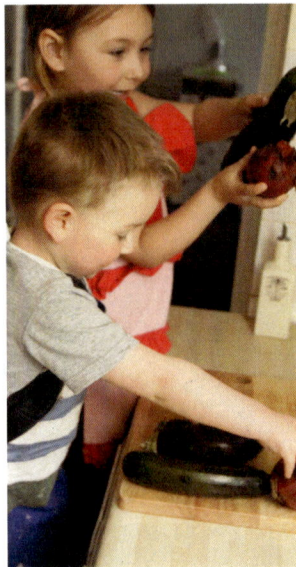

1. START BY GETTING ALL OF YOUR VEGETABLES OUT AND GIVING THEM A GOOD WASH. WHILST YOUR AT IT GIVE THEM A GOOD CHECK OVER TO MAKE SURE THEY ARE FRESH.

2. ONCE ALL OF THE VEGETABLES ARE READY ASK THE NEAREST BIG PERSON TO HELP CHOP THEM ALL UP.

THE AUBERGINES NEED CHOPPING UP INTO MEDIUM SIZED CHUNKS.

THE COURGETTES NEED SLICING UP INTO THICK CHUNKS.

THE RED ONIONS, PEPPERS AND THE TOMATOES JUST NEED ROUGHLY SLICING UP.

3. NOW YOUR BIG PERSON NEEDS TO GENTLY FRY THE INGREDIENTS. FIRST FRY THE AUBERGINES FOR 5 MINUTES BROWNING EACH SIDE NICELY. REMOVE FROM THE PAN AND SET TO ONE SIDE.

REPEAT THIS WITH THE COURGETTES AND PEPPERS BEING CAREFUL TO NOT OVER COOK THEM.

4. NOW FRY OFF THE CRUSHED GARLIC AND ADD ALL OF THE INGREDIENTS INCLUDING THE CHOPPED UP TOMATOES, RED WINE VINEGAR AND TORN UP BITS OF BASIL.

GIVE IT A GOOD STIR THEN ADD A TABLE SPOON OF SUGAR AND FRY FOR A FURTHER 5-8 MINUTES AND SERVE.

NOM NOM NOM!

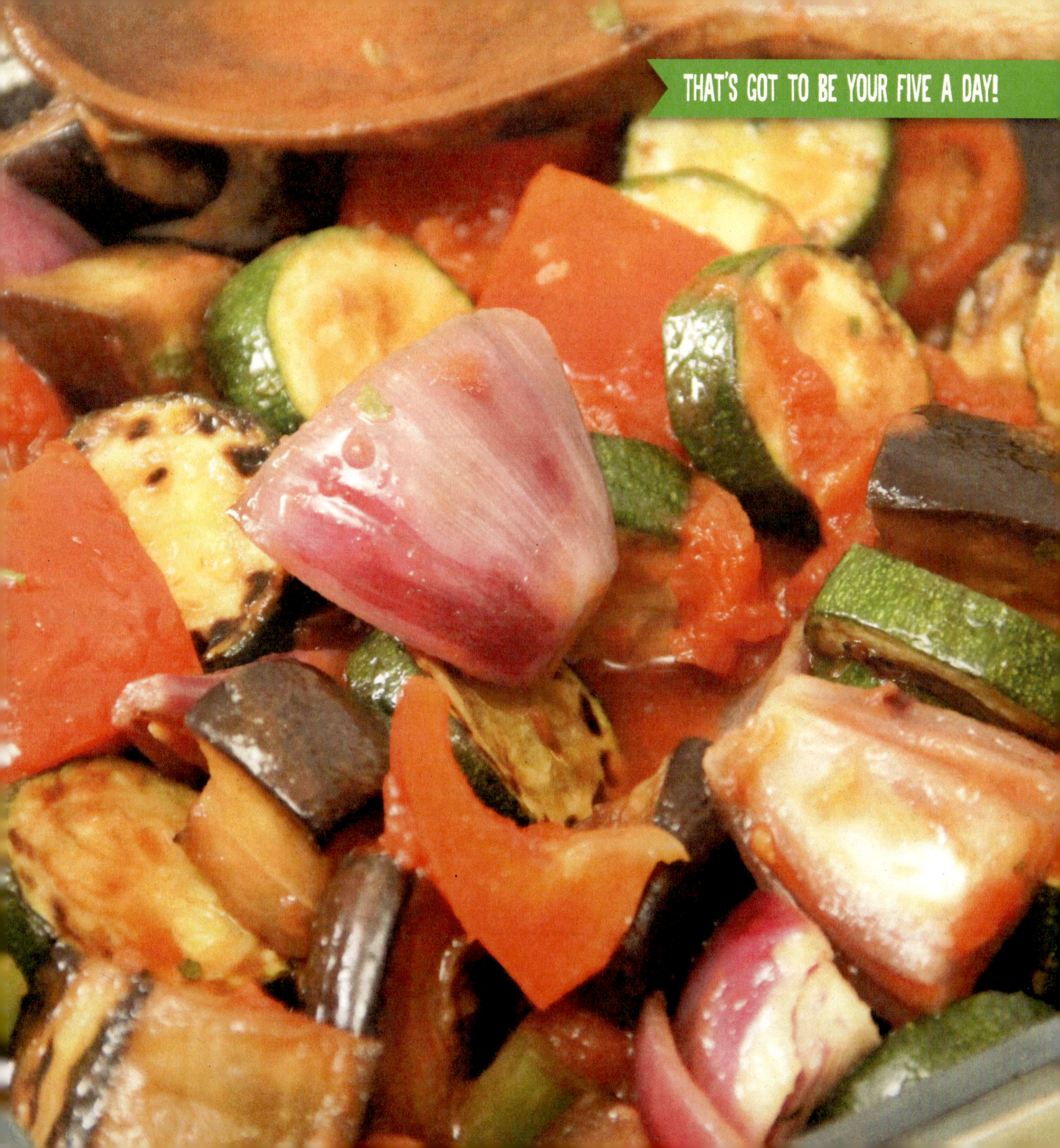
THAT'S GOT TO BE YOUR FIVE A DAY!

CANDY CANE REINDEERS

Prep: **10 MINS**

These simple delights are perfect tree decorations for as long as you can resist eating them!

Now I know that there is not technically any cooking in this recipe but ignore that, it's a whole lot of fun making these little treats and it's my book, my rules! The googly eyes are great and each reindeer ends up with so much character!

YOU WILL NEED:

SOME CANDY CANE STICKS
(CELLOPHANE WRAPPED ONES ARE IDEAL)

BROWN PIPE CLEANERS

A FEW RED BOBBLES

SOME GOOGLY EYES

A BLOB OR SO OF PVA GLUE
(ALL AVAILABLE AT MOST CRAFT SHOPS)

1. IT'S TIME TO GET CRAFTY! SO TAKE A BROWN PIPE CLEANER AND WRAP IT AROUND THE TOP OF THE CANDY CANE TO MAKE THE BASIS OF THE HEAD AND NECK.

NEXT TAKE A SECOND PIPE CLEANER AND WRAP IT AROUND THE TOP OF CANDY CANE AND TWIZZLE IT SO IT STAYS IN POSITION. YOU SHOULD HAVE 2 LONG BITS STICKING OUT FROM THE TOP OF THE CANDY CANE NOW. THESE CAN BE TWISTED AND BENT UNTIL THEY RESEMBLE ANTLERS.

2. ONCE YOU ARE HAPPY WITH THE ANTLERS, IT IS TIME TO ADD A NOSE AND EYES. USING A SMALL BLOB OF PVA GLUE, ATTACH THE RED BOBBLE TO THE NOW BROWN END OF THE CANDY CANE. USE THE SAME METHOD TO ATTACH THE EYES JUST IN FRONT OF THE ANTLERS.

3. THAT'S IT, JUST LET THE GLUE DRY FOR A BIT AND THEY ARE READY. YOU CAN TIE A STRING AROUND THEM TO HANG THEM FROM YOUR TREE AND WHEN YOU ARE READY TO EAT THEM JUST UNWRAP THE PLASTIC AND REMOVE THE REINDEER TO ENJOY THE TASTY CANDY CANES!

why not try a mammoth?!

STICKY TOFFEE PUDDING

Prep: **25 MINS**
Cooking: **45 MINS**

Another wintery delight, this traditional favourite is a sure winner

This family favourite dessert is best enjoyed in the winter when it's chilly outside and you need warming up! The beautiful rich taste will keep you going after the hardest of days!

YOU WILL NEED:

175G DATES, STONED AND ROUGHLY CHOPPED
1 TSP BICARBONATE OF SODA
300ML BOILING WATER
50G BUTTER
80G GOLDEN CASTER SUGAR
175G FLOUR
1 TSP BAKING POWDER
PINCH OF GROUND CLOVES
75G WALNUTS
80G DARK MUSCOVADO SUGAR
2 FREE RANGE EGGS

FOR THE SAUCE:
115G BUTTER
75G GOLDEN CASTER SUGAR
40G DARK MUSCOVADO SUGAR
140ML DOUBLE CREAM

1. RIGHT, WE WILL START WITH THE HOT BITS. YOUR BIG PERSON WILL NEED TO PREHEAT AN OVEN TO 190°C WHILE YOU GREASE A BAKING TIN.

THEN THEY NEED TO PLACE ALL OF THE SAUCE INGREDIENTS INTO A PAN AND BOIL FOR ABOUT 4 MINS STIRRING UNTIL IT REACHES A NICE STICKY CONSISTENCY.

2. POUR A THIRD OF THIS INTO THE TIN AND POP IT IN THE FREEZER TO SET.

3. WHILE THE BIG PEOPLE ARE USING WITH HEAT, ASK THEM TO ADD THE BOILING WATER TO A BOWL WITH THE DATES AND BICARBONATE OF SODA SO IT'S READY TO BE CAREFULLY MIXED THEN LEFT TO ONE SIDE.

A DELICIOUSLY SOFT SPONGE COVERED IN STICKY TOFFEE SAUCE!

4. RIGHT NOW US LITTLE PEOPLE CAN GET OUR HANDS DIRTY!

BEAT TOGETHER THE SUGAR AND BUTTER TO MAKE IT FLUFFY THEN BEAT IN THE EGGS.

THEN MIX IN THE FLOUR, BAKING POWDER, CLOVES AND A PINCH OF SALT. GIVE IT A GOOD MIX THEN ADD THE DATES AND WATER MIX ALONG WITH THE WALNUTS.

5. GET THE DISH OUT OF THE FREEZER AND POUR THIS NEW MIXTURE ON TOP OF THE TOFFEE SAUCE. POP IT IN THE OVEN FOR HALF AN HOUR. WHEN IT COMES OUT IT SHOULD BE QUITE FIRM.

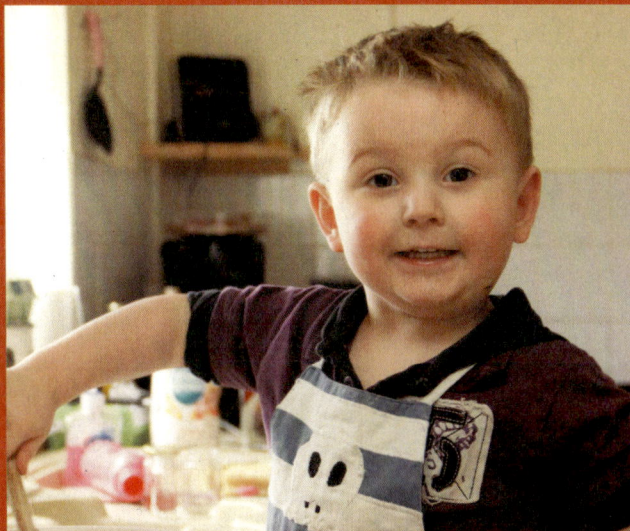

6. WHEN YOU ARE READY TO SERVE, HEAT UP THE REMAINING TOFFEE SAUCE AND POUR OVER THE PUDDING. SERVE GENEROUS PORTIONS WITH SOME SIMPLE VANILLA ICE CREAM FOR THAT LOVELY HOT AND COLD, STICKY TOFFEE GOODNESS!

REDCURRANT JELLY

Ok, it may not wobble but it's still jelly! kind of.

Prep: **30 MINS**
Cooking: **40 MINS**

This is a great recipe that makes a delicious jelly that can be used in many other great recipes! Especially good around Christmas time.

YOU WILL NEED:

900G FRESH RED CURRANTS
900G SUGAR
A MUSLIN SIEVE
STERILISED JAM JARS
WAX DISCS

1. SO START BY POURING ALL THE REDCURRANTS INTO A PRESERVING PAN. WHAT'S GREAT IS THAT YOU DON'T NEED TO REMOVE THE STALKS.

GIVE THEM A GOOD WASH AND REMOVE ANY BAD ONES THOUGH.

2. A BIG PERSON NEEDS TO POP THE PAN ON THE HEAT AND MIX AND PRESS THE CURRANTS TO GET THE WHOLE FLAVOUR OUT OF THEM, PROBABLY FOR ABOUT 10 MINUTES.

3. AFTER THIS TIME, ADD THE SUGAR.

LET THIS DISSOLVE THEN RAPIDLY BOIL THE MIXTURE FOR ABOUT 10 MINS.

143

FRESH REDCURRANT JELLY

4. NOW IT GETS MESSY! WHEN THE JELLY IS READY, POUR IT INTO THE MUSLIN SIEVE AND LET IT DRIP INTO A JAR.

THIS CAN TAKE A WHILE AND IT IS BEST TO LEAVE IT AS LONG AS POSSIBLE AS THE JELLY WILL BE CLEARER. YOU MAY NEED TO PUSH THE JELLY THROUGH AFTER A WHILE BUT A LITTLE PATIENCE WILL ACHIEVE A LOVELY CLEAR JELLY.

5. YOU NEED TO STERILISE YOUR JAM JARS IN THE OVEN. A BIG PERSON CAN DO THIS BY HEATING THE OVEN TO 140°C AND STERILISING THE JARS FOR 40 MINUTES.

WHEN THE JARS ARE HOT AND THE JELLY SIEVED, WE SPOONED THE JELLY INTO IT'S FINAL JARS.

ONCE IN THE JARS, COVER THE JELLY WITH THE WAX DISCS. THIS WILL KEEP FOR MONTHS AND YOU WILL BE SUPRISED HOW OFTEN YOU WILL USE IT NOW YOU KNOW YOU HAVE IT!

sometimes with just a little help...
you can do anything!